BECOMING A NEW YOU IN 30 DAYS!

WONDRA SPENCER

Copyright © 2024 Wondra Spencer.

All rights reserved. This book or any portion thereof may not be reproduced or used in any manner whatsoever without the express written permission of the publisher except for the use of brief quotations in a book review.

DEDICATION

To my loves: I want to send my book to my little cuties, Elijah and Eliana. Thanks for listening to me and keeping Mommy so happy. You brought joy to my life. Freddie, thanks for being a dear husband and a fantastic person.

Table of Contents

About and Contact the Author 1

Gift 3

About The Book 5

Introduction 7

Day 1 – Forgive and Love Yourself 9

Day 2 – Commit to Becoming a Better You (Self contract) 13

Day 3 – Meditation 21

Day 4 – Goals 27

Day 5 – Watch the Sunrise/Sunset 31

Day 6 – Drink More Water 33

Day 7 – Weekly Exercise Plan 35

Day 8 – Remove Negativity 41

Day 9 – Cooking Plan and Grocery Store Shopping 45

Day 10 – Date and Cleanse Your Skin 51

Day 11 – Date Your Mate 53

Day 12 – List What You Are Grateful For 57

Day 13 – Plan Events with Your Family 61

Day 14 – Dance and stretch for 30 mins 65

Day 15 – Have a Good Laugh and Enjoy a Great Movie! 69

Day 16 – Clean the Car & House 73

Day 17 – Pampering Day 81

Day 18 – No Excuses... 83

Day 19 – Step Out for a 15-Minute Nature Walk 85

Day 20 – Call a Positive Person 87

Day 21 – Rest Day and Positive Affirmations 89

Day 22 – Automate Savings and Retirement........................... 91

Day 23 – Disconnect and Unplug for 30 Minutes a Day 95

Day 24 – Forgive Others 99

Day 25 – Treat Your Body and Relax 103

Day 26 – Refrain from Eating Past 8 pm 107

Day 27 – Meditate in the am and Before Bed 109

Day 28 – Read an Enjoyable Book... 113

Day 29 – Complete Your To-do List 115

Day 30 – Limit Social Media.. 117

Celebration – Take time to Celebrate your Progress! 121

Plan of Action 129

About and Contact the Author

I'm thrilled to introduce you to Wondra Spencer, a native of Mobile, Alabama. As the eldest of three siblings, Wondra holds wisdom and kindness, which she eagerly shares to mentor others and infuse them with courage and charisma. As a respected United States Air Force veteran, Wondra brings her exceptional leadership skills into her roles as a devoted wife, a nurturing mother, and a highly skilled healthcare professional with over 20+ years of experience. Her degree in Health Information Management and her status as a Registered Health Information Technician (RHIT) speaks volumes about her expertise in the field. Wondra is a Master Life Coach.

Wondra is dedicated to her profession and deeply passionate about giving back to her community through volunteering and mentoring—her love for her family and friends and her penchant for reading, traveling, and embracing nature. Wondra has also authored the empowering "What is Your Motivation?" journal, available on www.wondraspencer.com, and a Yearly Gratitude Journal, which you can find on Amazon.com and www.wondraspencer.com.

Join Wondra on her incredible journey and discover an array of motivational goodies! Connect with her on Facebook, Instagram, TikTok, and YouTube for daily inspiration. Don't forget to check out the Inspire and Drive stores on Facebook and Instagram. Let's celebrate Wondra's fantastic story and join her uplifting community!

Gift

Before you go, Wondra would like to give you a special gift. You can claim your gift by visiting wondraspencer.com. The offer is available for a limited time, so check it out on Wondra's website at wondraspencer.com.

About The Book

Hey there, Motivators! I'm excited to tell you about this fantastic book that can help you transform into a new version of yourself in 30 days! It's all about empowering you to take charge of your growth. By completing the tasks in the book, you'll be on your way to an incredible personal transformation. The journey will be fundamental and rewarding.

Transforming yourself in just 30 days is an exciting challenge! Here are some steps you can take to start this journey:

1. **Set Clear Goals**: Define your goals in these 30 days. Be specific and realistic.

2. **Create a Plan**: Break down your goals into daily or weekly tasks. You can make them more manageable.

3. **Embrace Change**: Be open to new experiences and perspectives. Change can be uncomfortable, but it's essential for growth.

4. **Practice Mindfulness**: Spend a few minutes each day meditating or reflecting. It can help you stay focused and reduce stress.

5. **Stay Active**: Incorporate physical activity into your routine. Exercise boosts your mood and energy levels.

6. **Learn Something New**: Dedicate time to learning a new skill or hobby. It keeps your mind sharp and engaged.

7. **Connect with Others**: Build or strengthen relationships. Support from friends and family can be incredibly motivating.

8. **Reflect and Adjust**: Review your progress regularly and adjust as needed. Flexibility is vital to staying on track.

9. **Stay Positive**: Maintain a positive mindset. Celebrate small victories and learn from setbacks.

10. **Commit to Consistency**: Consistency is crucial. Stick to your plan and stay committed to your goals.

Let's do this together!

Introduction

Welcome! Take a moment to relax, envision a better version of yourself, and consider the possibilities for improving your overall well-being. Have you ever woken up feeling like you could use a fresh start, eager to embrace positive transformations? I am thrilled to share an incredible book called "Becoming a New You in 30 Days." Wondra's book is an all-encompassing guide to reshaping your mindset, enhancing your health, and rejuvenating your body. Its valuable insights and practical techniques benefit you and extend to your loved ones and colleagues. It is a powerful tool for anyone on a journey of personal growth and positive change. You can inspire both yourself and those around you. Let's embark on this exciting journey together!

DAY 1

Forgive and Love Yourself

Forgiveness and self-love are naturally linked - the ability to forgive ourselves is a profound act of self-compassion that allows us to let go of guilt, shame, and regret and embrace the totality of who we are. You can be an accountable person to yourself before you can assist anyone else. Too often, we are our own harshest critics, endlessly criticizing ourselves for our perceived flaws and shortcomings. We hold ourselves to impossibly high standards, unable to show ourselves the same kindness and understanding we so freely extend to others. But true self-acceptance means acknowledging our humanity - we are imperfect, vulnerable beings who will inevitably make mistakes and have moments of weakness. We open the door to profound healing and growth when we meet those imperfections with empathy rather than judgment. Self-forgiveness is an ongoing practice, a daily choice to let go of self-criticism and embrace the fullness of our positive and negative experiences. And from that solid foundation of self-love, we become more capable of extending that same grace to the world around us. When we learn to treat ourselves with the respect, kindness, and unconditional positive regard we deserve, we become a wellspring of compassion - a living testament to the transformative power of forgiveness and self-acceptance.

Forgiving and loving yourself is such an important journey. It cannot be overlooked. It's about recognizing your imperfections and understanding that everyone makes mistakes. Start by acknowledging your feelings, then practice self-compassion. Treat yourself with the same kindness you'd offer a friend. Remember, you're a work in progress, and that's perfectly okay. You want to take it one step further: forgive and love yourself. It is only one of you, and you must love yourself!

Day one, forgive yourself. It would be best if you did not go on this new journey in life and didn't have the chance to forgive yourself. You want to forgive yourself and give yourself back that power because no one can take that power away from you ever again. The days and experiences I share in this book are dear and close to my heart because I practiced the same techniques throughout my life. I will share these techniques with my friends, family, coworkers, and strangers.

I want to share these helpful techniques with the world and with others. These techniques can be used as learning tools whether you are an adolescent, teenager, or adult in your senior years.

It is time to forgive yourself for putting yourself down. I do not want you to do that and stop immediately! Please list the negative things on paper, take them, tear them up, and throw them away. You have released the negativity. Please list the positive things on paper, take them, put them somewhere safe, and leave them. You can reference the positive updates whenever you like.

Make sure you say your positive affirmations daily and compliment yourself daily. When you go outside for a quick errand, look good. Shower, brush your teeth, and wash your hair to look good. You can teach your kids the same.

How to Love Yourself:

- Find out why you do not love yourself.
- Add it to your negative thoughts.
- Replace it with a positive thought.

Loving yourself is a journey that involves a few essential practices. Listed below are nine suggestions:

1. **Practice Self-Compassion:** Treat yourself with kindness, especially when struggling. Acknowledge your feelings without judgment.

2. **Set Boundaries:** Protect your energy by saying no to things that drain you and yes to what uplifts you.

3. **Celebrate Your Strengths:** Focus on your achievements and what makes you unique. Keep a list of things you love about yourself.

4. **Take Care of Your Body:** Eat healthy food, exercise, and rest. Your body is your home, so treat it well.

5. **Engage in Activities You Enjoy:** Make time for hobbies and interests that bring you joy and fulfillment.

6. **Surround Yourself with Positivity:** Spend time with supportive people who lift you and encourage your growth.

7. **Practice Mindfulness:** Be present in the moment. Meditation or deep breathing can help you connect with yourself.

8. **Challenge Negative Self-Talk:** Notice when you're being hard on yourself and replace those thoughts with affirming ones.

9. **Seek Help if Needed:** If you're struggling, consider talking to a life coach, therapist, or counselor for support.

Remember, loving yourself is a continuous process. Be patient and gentle with yourself along the way! Remove the toxic people and things in your life because they will weigh you down. Get to know yourself because you are unique, intelligent, loving, and kind. And keep on loving yourself!

For example, forgive yourself and no worries. It will release many unwanted feelings.

DAY 2

Commit to Becoming a Better You (Self contract)

Committing to becoming a better version of yourself is a powerful and transformative journey that requires introspection and action. It is being open and having an honest self-assessment - recognizing your strengths, weaknesses, and areas for growth. From here, you must craft a personalized "self-contract" - a detailed plan that outlines specific, measurable goals and the concrete steps you will take to achieve them. It might involve developing a new skill, breaking a harmful habit, or cultivating a positive mindset. Self-contract is a guiding light, helping you stay focused and accountable as you navigate the ebbs and flows of personal growth. Of course, becoming a "better you" are not a one-time destination but an ongoing process of self-improvement. There will be challenges and setbacks, but each small victory builds momentum and strength. With each milestone reached, you'll experience the immense satisfaction of watching your aspirations become reality. The valid reward is itself - the profound sense of fulfillment that comes from dedicating yourself to becoming the best possible version of who you are. By honoring your self-contract and fully committing to this transformative process, you unlock your full potential and cultivate the wisdom, strength, and joy that define a life well-lived.

When you make a personal commitment, it carries a significant weight that compels you to honor it, even in challenging times. It's not just about facing the repercussions of breaking the commitment; it's also about the fact that you willingly agreed to it when you first made it. When you make a promise, whether a casual agreement or a formal contract, I strive to uphold it. Most people are reluctant to renege on their commitments, especially those documented in a contract.

Our brains drive us to align our actions with our beliefs, so signing a contract alters our perception of an agreement. It transforms a document with guidelines into something you have actively committed to. As a result, your mind will exert maximum effort to adhere to the terms of the contract, even if it's a self-imposed one.

If the idea of a self-contract seems daunting, fear not. The beauty of a self-contract is that it simplifies your life. It outlines your goals, what needs to be done, and how to do it, providing clarity on your personal goals.

Before I discuss self-contract, I want you to go to your favorite place, grab your favorite pen, laptop, paper, or electronic device, and think about your contract to yourself. It will allow you to delve deeper into before writing about the contract.

Here is a sample of a personalized contract you can create. Your contract helps you commit to specific actions and steps to improve your overall well-being, focusing on weight management and personal development. By including your full name and the current date on the contract, you can formalize your commitment to yourself.

After creating the contract, store it in a meaningful location. It could be anywhere easily accessible and constantly remind you of your commitment.

Consider placing it on your refrigerator, in your favorite book, in your handbag, or in a location that is significant to you.

When drafting the contract, remember some tips to simplify the process. Focus on a single goal to avoid distractions, write down precise and straightforward steps to achieve the goal, set a short deadline, and keep the contract brief and formal. Emphasize the positive actions and outcomes, remember to modify the agreement as needed, and celebrate your achievements. Rewarding yourself after reaching each goal is important to stay motivated.

When you make a personal commitment, it carries a significant weight that compels you to honor it, even in challenging times. It's not just about facing the repercussions of breaking the commitment; it's also about the fact that you willingly agreed to it when you first made it. When you make a promise, whether a casual agreement or a formal contract, I strive to uphold it. Most people are reluctant to renege on their commitments, especially those documented in a contract.

Our brains drive us to align our actions with our beliefs, so signing a contract alters our perception of an agreement. It transforms a document with guidelines into something you have actively committed to. As a result, your mind will exert maximum effort to adhere to the terms of the contract, even if it's a self-imposed one.

If the idea of a self-contract seems daunting, fear not. The beauty of a self-contract is that it simplifies your life. It identifies your goals, what needs to be done, and how to do it, clarifying your personal goals.

Here is a sample of a personalized contract you can create. This contract helps you commit to specific actions and steps to improve your overall well-being, focusing on weight management and personal development. By including your full name and the current date on the contract, you can formalize your commitment to yourself.

Here's an example of how you can structure your self-contract:

- Full Name: [Your Full Name]

- Date: [Current Date]

- Goal: [Specific Goal Related to Weight Management or Personal Development]

- Consequences of not meeting my goal: [Consequences you set for yourself]

- Rewards/reinforcements for meeting my goal: [Rewards or treats for yourself]

- Completion Date: [Your Deadline]

- Signature and Date: [Your Signature and Date]

Let's prepare in advance and devise strategies to overcome any obstacles that may come our way.

We've all attempted to talk our way out of a traffic ticket or school penalty at some point. It's just as important to approach our self-contract with the same level of preparation. By planning and outlining how we'll handle decisions, we can make thoughtful choices rather than allowing emotions to dictate our actions.

Consider introducing repercussions if you need help to meet your commitments consistently. Having an accountability partner or group can be a powerful motivator. Whether you decide to wager real money or put your reputation on the line (including using an app that publicly discloses any slip-ups), the added pressure can be a significant incentive to stick to your goals.

Formalize your commitment by writing and signing your self-contract. There's something undeniably definitive about putting pen to paper and signing your name. It modifies your pledge, and you could display the contract prominently on your desk for extra reinforcement.

Seek out a trusted co-signer if you need additional support. If you're concerned about staying true to your commitments, having someone else sign the contract with you can provide valuable reinforcement. Whether it's a close friend, mentor, or respected colleague, having a co-signer with your best interests at heart can ensure you remain on track.

Make your commitment public to hold yourself accountable. Sharing your commitment with others can be a powerful motivator. Not only does it create a sense of responsibility to avoid letting others down, but it also reinforces your determination to honor a public promise.

Enlist the encouragement of friends and family to support you. There's no better source of encouragement than those closest to you. The optional weight of a contract can become lighter with the support of friends and family, who can offer invaluable cheerleading throughout your journey.

Connect with a community of individuals pursuing similar objectives. Joining a small group of individuals facing similar challenges can provide a sense of camaraderie and solidarity. You'll receive support and guidance from those who understand your journey and can offer assistance if you encounter any setbacks.

Keep track of your progress to ensure you're moving toward your objectives. Consistently documenting your progress, whether completing tasks or acknowledging your daily accomplishments, is crucial for staying on course. You have tangible evidence that you're making strides toward your personal goals.

Now that you've signed your self-contract, it's time to implement your plan! Consider your self-contract a roadmap for accomplishing your goals, a trustworthy companion that will help you remain accountable to yourself. You want to live your best life! Remember, once you create this contract, you can edit or end it as needed.

Embrace Your Routine: You'll reap the benefits once you establish your daily routine.

Routines can be fulfilling and enjoyable, and their health advantages may make you wonder why you didn't start one earlier. They can help reduce stress, improve sleep, promote healthier eating, encourage exercise, and enhance cognitive function. I've designed this daily routine to be concise and impactful. If you're ready to delve deeper, explore my coaching packages at wondraspencer.com. We can collaborate on improving your health and wellness, and I can help keep you motivated!

Steps:

- Wake Up
- Get Up
- Brush Teeth

- Exercise in am
- Take a Shower
- Get Dressed
- Get up kids
- Cook and have Breakfast by 9a
- Take the Kids to school or wait for the school bus (If you don't have kids, ensure your mate is ok)
- Go to work
- Meetings
- Eat lunch between 12p-1p
- Go back home
- Cook dinner
- Help kids with homework
- Eat dinner
- Exercise in pm
- Shower
- Watch tv/social media
- Go to bed and reset

It is a great way to rest and decompress your day and reconvene for the next day.

DAY 3

Meditation

Meditation has been a powerful practice for centuries to cultivate inner peace, focus the mind, and foster greater self-awareness. Meditation involves sitting quietly and directing one's attention inward, often focusing on the breath or a mantra. Meditation can tap into a deep well of calm and clarity within by stilling the mind and turning inward. Regular meditation can reduce stress and anxiety, improve concentration and cognitive function, and even alter the structure and function of the brain over time. As one delves deeper into the practice, meditation can also become a gateway to profound insights about the nature of consciousness, the self, and one's place in the grand scheme. Indeed, many spiritual and religious traditions view meditation as transcending the ego and connecting it with a higher power or universal source of being. Whether approached from a secular or spiritual perspective, the transformative potential of meditation lies in its ability to quiet the incessant chatter of the mind and anchor us firmly in the peaceful present moment. With dedicated practice, the benefits of meditation can radiate out to enrich every facet of one's life, from relationships and work to overall health and well-being.

Beginning your day with meditation is an excellent choice. Daily meditation can improve your stress, anxiety, and overall mental well-being. If you try it, please share your experience in the book reviews, on www.wondraspencer.com website, on social media, and with others.

When you practice meditation, you will experience a sense of clarity. Once you explore meditation, you will understand. It is a method of mindfulness and awareness of your surroundings. In addition, it is the best technique for your brain. It will remind you to concentrate on your day and thoughts, help you breathe, and get through any challenges in your life.

Meditation is for everyone, regardless of age, background, or experience level. Here are a few reasons why it's so accessible:

- **No Special Skills Required:** You don't need any prior experience to start. Just a willingness to try is enough.

- **Flexible Practices:** There are many types of meditation—mindfulness, loving-kindness, guided, or movement-based practices like yoga—to find what resonates with you.

- **Short-Time Commitment:** A few minutes daily can make a difference. You can meditate briefly during a break or have longer sessions at home.

- **Variety of Resources:** There are countless apps, videos, and classes available to guide you, making it easier to start.

- **Adaptable to Your Needs**: Meditation can be tailored to address specific needs, like stress relief, emotional regulation, or enhancing focus.

- **Community Support:** Many people find encouragement in groups in person or online, which can enhance the experience. Meditation can benefit anyone looking for more peace, clarity, and self-awareness.

Below is a listing of ten reasons you should meditate, such as understanding your pain, reducing your stress levels, connecting better in your life, improving your focus, enhancing your brain, reducing emotional stress, self-sufficiency, better sleep, boosting your immune system, and improving your mental status.

Here are ten reasons to meditate:

1. **Embracing the Power of Meditation:** By practicing meditation, you can gain a profound awareness of your physical and emotional pain, empowering you to address it with clarity and compassion.

2. **Elevate Your Well-being:** Consistent meditation has significantly lowered stress levels, paving the way for a calmer and more relaxed daily experience.

3. **Forge Deeper Connections:** Meditation is a powerful tool for enhancing mindfulness and empathy, enriching relationships and communication with others, and fostering more profound connections.

4. **Sharpen Your Focus:** Through meditation, you can effectively train your mind to concentrate better, enhancing your focus and productivity.

5. **Quieten the Mind:** Through meditation, you can experience the tranquility of a quieter mind and a decluttered mental space, leading to greater peace and clarity.

6. **Nurture Emotional Well-being:** Meditation can uplift your mood and perspective, nurturing a more positive and balanced mindset.

7. **Cultivate Self-Awareness:** Meditation allows you to delve deeper into your thoughts, emotions, and behaviors, fostering greater self-understanding and personal growth.

8. **Embrace Restorative Sleep:** Meditation can improve sleep quality by calming the mind and body and making it easier to drift into a restful slumber.

9. **Strengthen Your Immunity:** Regular meditation can fortify your immune system, bolstering your body's ability to resist illness and recover swiftly.

10. **Foster Mental Strength:** Embrace meditation's empowering effects on building mental strength, which will equip you to navigate life's challenges and setbacks more easily.

Below is the link to the guided meditation with Wondra.

https://www.youtube.com/watch?v=f4eDtts3P1U&t=122s

Quick meditation Guide

Welcome to a guided meditation with Wondra

Starting your day with meditation is a great choice, and I am happy to guide you through it.

Begin by finding a comfortable seated position and resting your hands on your knees, with palms facing upwards.

Take three deep breaths, exhaling through your open mouth.

Next, take a moment to express gratitude for everything you have today and focus on what you're thankful for.

Breathe in positive energy, imagine it entering your body through the top of your head, and do this three times.

As you breathe out, imagine that positive energy flowing through your body, down to your limbs, and out through the tips of your toes, washing away any negative thoughts, energy, and emotions that do not serve you.

Take three deep breaths, exhaling through your open mouth.

Next, take a moment to express gratitude for everything you have today and focus on what you're thankful for.

Breathe in positive energy and imagine it entering your body through the top of your head.

As you breathe out, imagine that positive energy flowing through your body, down to your limbs, and out through the tips of your toes, washing away any negative thoughts, energy, and emotions that do not serve you.

Continue this visualization for a few more deep breaths.

Finally, take three final breaths with an open mouth and exhale. You are now ready to begin your day as your highest self. Blink open your eyes and see the world from a fresh perspective. Have a wonderful day! Namaste.

DAY 4

Goals

Goals are the targets or aims that individuals or organizations strive to achieve. They provide a sense of purpose, direction, and motivation, driving us to act and push ourselves to greater heights. Whether it's a personal goal to learn a new skill, a professional goal to advance in one's career, or a broader societal goal to address a pressing issue, goals give us something to work toward and a clear vision of what we hope to accomplish. You should set achievable, measurable goals, which are crucial for tracking progress, celebrating milestones, and adjusting strategies. Goals can be short-term, like completing a project by the end of the week, or long-term, like saving up to buy a house in the next five years. They may be concrete and tangible, such as increasing sales by 20% this quarter, or more abstract, like finding greater fulfillment and work-life balance. Regardless of the specifics, goals inspire us to grow, challenge ourselves, and ultimately realize our full potential. By establishing clear goals and remaining steadfast in pursuing them, we can transform our dreams into reality and make meaningful, lasting changes in our lives and the world around us.

It is time to bring out your contract and look at your goals. Now is the time to review your goals and ensure you have executed them. It is the time to revise your goals, think about them, and enhance them. Do you want your goals to be innovative? With the goals, you want to make sure that you can count them and that they will be able to reference them in the future.

Goals are the targets or aims that individuals or organizations strive to achieve. They provide a sense of purpose, direction, and motivation, driving us to act and push ourselves to greater heights. Whether it's a personal goal to learn a new skill, a professional goal to advance in one's career, or a broader societal goal to address a pressing issue, goals give us something to work toward and a clear vision of what we hope to accomplish. You should set achievable, measurable goals, which are crucial for tracking progress, celebrating milestones, and adjusting strategies. Goals can be short-term, like completing a project by the end of the week, or long-term, like saving up to buy a house in the next five years. They may be concrete and tangible, such as increasing sales by 20% this quarter, or more abstract, like finding greater fulfillment and work-life balance. Regardless of the specifics, goals inspire us to grow, challenge ourselves, and ultimately realize our full potential. By establishing clear goals and remaining steadfast in pursuing them, we can transform our dreams into reality and make meaningful, lasting changes in our lives and the world around us.

Your yearly goals shouldn't be dreadful! I write my plans in January and read the previous year's goals. If needed, I will continue them and celebrate my accomplishments. For instance, once I completed my degree, I bought one of my favorites. My favorites are lovely handbags, a spa date with myself, and an enjoyable family vacation. Meanwhile, I have a spa date every year on my birthday. It is one of my self-care dates.

My favorite part of a family vacation is having unlimited time to relax with the family.

I selected goals for my family because they might have plans for themselves, and I can continue to have unique goals for them. My goal for my family is to have them be healthy and live a relevant life. Sometimes, your family is not thinking about their goals, but you can instill goodness in them. Don't stop pursuing your goals under any circumstances!

Setting goals can be incredibly beneficial for personal growth and well-being. Here are some reasons why having goals is good for you:

- **Direction and Focus:** Goals give you a clear sense of purpose and direction, helping you prioritize your time and energy.

- **Motivation:** Having something to strive for can motivate you to overcome challenges and stay engaged.

- **Measure Progress:** Goals allow you to track your achievements, boost your confidence, and provide a sense of accomplishment.

- **Improved Decision-Making:** When you have clear goals, making choices that align with your values and aspirations becomes easier.

- **Personal Growth:** Setting and pursuing goals often leads to new skills and experiences, fostering personal development.

- **Increased Stability:** Working towards goals can help you develop perseverance and adaptability in the face of setbacks.

- **Enhanced Well-Being:** Achieving goals can increase happiness and satisfaction, especially when they align with your values.

Set specific, measurable, achievable, relevant, and time-bound goals (SMART).

It is time to bring out your contract and look at your goals. Now is the time to review your goals and ensure you have executed them. It is the time to revise your goals, think about them, and enhance them. Do you want your goals to be innovative? With the goals, you want to make sure that you can count on them and that they can reference them in the future.

Meditate for 15 minutes.

SMART Goal: I will set aside 15 minutes daily to sit in silence and focus on my breath. I will not get distracted by my family, thoughts, and noises. If there are any distractions, I will restart my meditation process.

Specific: You have a particular action and will sit silently and focus on your breath.

Measurable: You can track your daily meditation time in your What Is Your Motivation Journal.

Attainable: Sitting quietly for 15 minutes is a realistic and achievable goal.

Relevant: Stress leads to being overweight, and reducing my stress is a way to lose weight.

Time-based: I will maintain my daily meditation goal of reducing stress and becoming healthier.

DAY 5

Watch the Sunrise/Sunset

Watching the sunrise or sunset is a breathtaking experience connecting us to the world's natural rhythms. As the sun dips below the horizon or slowly ascends into the sky, the sky erupts in a magnificent display of vibrant colors - fiery oranges, deep reds, and brilliant pinks that paint the clouds in stunning natural artwork. Watching the sunrise is such a peaceful experience. The colors change in the sky, and the world wakes up—it's like nature's way of reminding us to pause and appreciate the moment.

Witnessing this daily celestial event is a grounding and humbling experience, reminding us of our place in the universe's grand scheme. Whether the first golden rays of dawn peeking over the treetops or the final embers of dusk fading into the night, these transitional moments between night and day hold a special kind of magic. The shifting light casts everything in a warm, ethereal glow, transforming the most mundane landscapes into a scene of pure beauty. And in those fleeting minutes, we are invited to pause, take a deep breath, and marvel at the wonder of it all - the cyclical nature of the sun's journey, the interplay of light and shadow, the vastness of the sky meeting the earth. Witnessing a sunrise or sunset is a chance to slow down, disconnect from the busyness of daily life, and connect with something greater than ourselves, reminding us of the simple, profound joys that can be found in nature's daily display.

It is incredible watching the sunset or the sunrise; it is soothing. If you are an early riser, watching the sunrise will be unique because you are up early. You might be getting your kids in order or getting your spouse or family member together. You can add this beautiful idea to your day. Watching the sunset will be fantastic if you are a late riser. Watch the sunset with me; you have completed your day. You've made sure that your day ended on a good note. Why are you watching the sunrise or sunset? Invite a friend, your family members, or someone close to you.

I like sunsets more because they have many variations in color and the sky overall. Sunsets can be equally breathtaking! How the sky transforms into a canvas of oranges, pinks, and purples is magical. It's such an excellent time to reflect on the day. Also, I can't wake up early enough to watch the sunrise. If you prefer sunrise because it is a new beginning, it will fill you with joy and energy for the day ahead.

DAY 6

Drink More Water

Staying properly hydrated is one of the most important, yet often overlooked, aspects of maintaining good health. Drinking an adequate amount of water each day is crucial for the body to function at its best. Water makes up about 60% of our body weight and serves countless vital functions, from regulating body temperature and cushioning joints to aiding digestion and flushing toxins. Unfortunately, many people fail to drink enough water, leading to many potential issues. Dehydration can cause fatigue, headaches, muscle cramps, and impaired cognitive function. The body's organs and cells can only correctly perform their duties with sufficient water intake.

Conversely, staying hydrated provides a wealth of benefits. Drinking water can boost metabolism, improve skin complexion, and even aid in weight loss by making you feel like you are not as hungry as usual. Additionally, proper hydration links and reduces the risk of certain diseases like kidney stones and some cancers. Given water's central role in human biology, experts recommend drinking at least eight 8-ounce glasses daily, though individual needs may vary based on factors like activity level, climate, and health conditions. People can enjoy optimal hydration's myriad physical and mental advantages by consciously drinking more water throughout the day.

Drink more water with any workout, and ensure you drink enough. If you are not drinking enough water, your body will hurt, and you will not be able to complete your workout. Water helps your muscles recover quickly and prevents dehydration while working out. It will also make your skin look better.

Drinking water before exercise is crucial for five several reasons:

1. **Hydration:** Staying hydrated helps maintain optimal bodily functions and performance during workouts.

2. **Temperature Regulation:** Water helps regulate body temperature, preventing overheating.

3. **Joint Lubrication:** Proper hydration supports joint function and reduces the risk of injuries.

4. **Energy Levels:** Being well-hydrated can enhance endurance and reduce fatigue.

5. **Digestive Health:** Hydration aids in digestion and nutrient absorption, which is essential for energy during exercise.

For the best results, aim to drink water 30 minutes to an hour before your workout.

You can grab your favorite water bottle to hold the water you need. We live in a digital world where you can monitor your water intake via laptop, workstation, application, and personal device.

DAY 7

Weekly Exercise Plan

All right, I hope you're still there with me. A well-structured weekly exercise plan is essential for maintaining a healthy and active lifestyle. Find the exercise you love and let it flow! Finding an exercise, you love is about exploring different activities until something resonates. Try various options like dancing, hiking, swimming, or team sports. Pay attention to what makes you feel energized and happy, and let that guide your routine. Enjoy the process, and let it flow!

The foundation of such a plan typically involves a balanced mix of different workout routines spread out over the course of the week. It could include cardiovascular exercises like jogging, swimming, or cycling on some days, paired with strength training sessions focused on building muscle and improving overall body tone on others. High-intensity interval training (HIIT) workouts that alternate short bursts of maximal effort with recovery periods are also a popular addition, as they can efficiently boost metabolism and burn fat. Flexibility and mobility work, such as Yoga or Pilates, might be incorporated to enhance range of motion, joint health, and overall balance. Rest and recovery days are just as crucial, allowing the body to repair and rebuild between more strenuous sessions. By strategically planning this weekly schedule, individuals can ensure they are challenging their bodies in diverse ways, targeting all the major muscle groups and physiological systems to achieve their fitness goals, whether improved cardiovascular fitness, increased strength, weight management, or simply feeling their best. A well-rounded weekly exercise plan can become a transformative part of one's lifestyle with dedication and consistency.

Exercise is essential for several reasons:

1. **Physical Health:** It strengthens the heart, muscles, and bones, reducing the risk of chronic diseases like diabetes and heart disease.

2. **Mental Well-Being:** Regular physical activity boosts mood, reduces anxiety, and can alleviate symptoms of depression.

3. **Weight Management:** Exercise helps maintain a healthy weight by burning calories and increasing metabolism.

4. **Increased Energy:** Regular activity improves stamina and energy levels.

5. **Better Sleep:** Exercise can improve sleep quality and duration.

6. **Social Interaction:** Group activities and classes can foster social connections and community.

7. **Cognitive Benefits:** Physical activity is linked to better brain health and memory.

Incorporating regular exercise into your routine can enhance your overall quality of life.

This day five will help you create your exercise. Before you make your exercise plan, please work with a provider to ensure that you are in great shape to do the exercise. Because I do not want anyone to hurt themselves, doing some training in the long run will help. I hope this brightens your day! I've been exercising in the nice weather, and usually, I wear okay clothes. I put on a cute exercise outfit and put music in my headphones. I thought I was pretty and walked for over an hour. I was shocked by it; I was sweaty and cute at the same time. If you wear a cute outfit and work out, it will be entertaining and motivation to exercise because you are pretty and getting healthier.

So, the exercise goal is a 30-minute nonstop workout. Do you want to ensure you have had enough water the day before you work out? The reason why is that I do not want you to be dehydrated. It is hard to keep back to normal. Before you work out, contact a family member, friend, neighbors, you can get others involved, but do not get discouraged if you work out alone because you will see results. You want to stretch before you do any workout and cool down at the end of your workout. With your exercise, I suggest doing something on Monday that will motivate you, such as a 30-minute walk around and it will increase your blood pressure and heart rate.

On Tuesday, I want you to do 20 squats, 20 crunches, and 20 pushups. Now, with 20 squats in the beginning, you can do regular squats, but you can take a weight for a 10-pound weight to the 20 squats. I want you to crunch on the floor or stand up. You can do your 20 pushups with pushup support, or you can do them on the floor, or you can do 20 pushups. Okay, Wednesday, you have done a great work out and pat yourself on the back, and you can keep going!

You can go to your favorite place to dance or turn up the volume in your headphones for those 30 minutes. You're getting a sweat out of your workout. Okay, it's Thursday, so you have one more day of working out, which is fantastic! On Thursday, you might have to push yourself a little because you're tired and your body does not want to work out. It is a new routine. You want to stick with the routine. On Thursday, if it takes you 30 minutes to complete this workout. It is okay. I want you to do ten jumping jacks. The fire hydrants will be nice because it is on the floor, and you can do 10. Lifting a 10-pound weight will help your muscles look better, but if you want it to do anything more significant, ensure you talk to your provider. The water will recover your muscles.

It's a great day because you should pat yourself on the back during the first week of working out. It is Friday and yoga time. You want to do yoga for 30 minutes. Yoga poses like the Downward-Facing Dog, Chair Pose, and Tree Pose are great for weight loss, and practicing them for 20 minutes can be effective in shedding pounds.

I want to share a little story with you. I have two younger kids, and my son likes to run track, so he told me he wanted to exercise, so I said OKAY. Initially, I couldn't exercise with him, so I walked with my family. As my body felt better over time, I could exercise with him. I am exercising with my family during the week. My workout partners are my family; we go to any part of the house, gym, or park and work out. During the workout sessions, my youngest runs around and tries her best to exercise. We love it! My husband and I love it because we, as a family, are trying to get and stay fit! You'll have the workout plan at the end of this chapter, and it works.

Sample Schedule

Hey there! Here's a fantastic weekly workout plan for you. Take 30 minutes to look and feel your best. I hope you can get your best and lovely outfits, proper shoes, water bottles, and electronics with your favorite artist.

Beginner:

When you are getting back into exercise, consult a provider and get cleared to exercise. Once the provider clears, you can get ready to walk. The first month is five days; try to walk with your exercise shoes, outfit, and bottled water. Before and after your walk, do an invigorating stretch. The stretch will prepare your body for walking. I want you to walk your best for 30 minutes. Newer moms, dads, and families put the kids in their strollers and have them enjoy nature. You want to do your relaxing cooldown for two minutes. It will ensure you will not injure yourself, enhance blood flow, and reduce the stressors on your body, such as heart and muscles. Once you feel reasonable, you can complete the advanced workout. You will still walk, but it can incorporate walking, running, yoga, weights, and other exercises.

Advance Workout:

Monday: Start the week with invigorating stretching, cardio (walking/running), and a relaxing cooldown.

Tuesday: Get ready to crush it with stretching, 20 squats, sit-ups/crunches, pushups, and a soothing cool down.

Wednesday: It's time to groove with energizing dancing and a rejuvenating cooldown.

Thursday: Let's power through with stretching, ten jumping jacks, a Fire hydrant, butt kicks, and a set of lifting 10-pound weights, then cool down and stretch.

Friday: Wrap up the week with calming stretching, a revitalizing Yoga session, and a soothing cool down. You've got this!

The weekends are a chance to hydrate and rest your body.

DAY 8

Remove Negativity

Removing negativity from one's life is crucial to achieving greater happiness, fulfillment, and overall well-being. It involves actively identifying and addressing the negative thought patterns, emotions, and external influences that can weigh us down and hinder our progress. This process begins with self-awareness - reflecting on our inner dialogue and recognizing when we engage in self-criticism, pessimism, or catastrophizing. By becoming more mindful of these opposing tendencies, we can then work to reframe our perspectives, challenge irrational beliefs, and cultivate a more positive and constructive mindset. It may involve practices such as journaling, meditation, or seeking the support of a therapist or counselor. There are many ways to attend sessions, such as in-person, remote, virtual, or electronic devices.

Negativity can lead to a range of issues, both for individuals and groups. It can foster stress, anxiety, and decreased motivation, which may result in poor mental and physical health. In relationships, negativity can create conflict and distance, undermining trust and communication. On a broader scale, a hostile atmosphere in workplaces or communities can stifle creativity, collaboration, and overall productivity. Finding ways to reframe from negativity into constructive thoughts can help mitigate these effects!

It is never too late to stop dreaming. But have you thought about making your dreams a reality? If you make your dreams a reality, you feel great about yourself and your accomplishments. We only live once and make the most of it! Because it is NEVER too late to make dreams come true. My grandmother Hilda said, Wondra, take one class a semester and achieve your career goals. I didn't listen initially, but before she passed away in 2014, I earned my Associate's degree in Health Information Management and obtained my Registered Health Information Management certification. I was so happy I had achieved my goal; she knew it! Along the way, I removed non-supporters from my team's circle and stuck to my plans. You can do the same!

Additionally, removing negativity can require an examination of our social circles and environments and making the difficult but necessary decision to distance ourselves from individuals or situations that breed toxicity and drain our energy. Replacing these with more uplifting relationships, activities, and sources of inspiration can have a profoundly transformative effect. Ultimately, removing negativity is an ongoing process of self-discovery, self-acceptance, and the conscious cultivation of a life aligned with our highest values and aspirations. It is a courageous act of self-care that empowers us to live with greater authenticity, spirit, and joy.

You want to remove the negativity in your life because if you do not, you will not be able to focus on your goals. If you cannot focus on your goals, then you will not be successful with yourself. One way to remove negativity from your life is therapy. There is still time to see a therapist.

Therapy can be a powerful tool for healing. It provides a safe space to explore thoughts and emotions, helping individuals understand their experiences and develop coping strategies. Through various therapeutic approaches, people can work through trauma, improve their relationships, and build resilience. Many find that therapy helps them heal and fosters personal growth and self-awareness. Finding a therapist who resonates with you can make a big difference! In the past, I have individuals shared that they would not go to therapy, but they needed it. It was not comforting because the individual needed it.

You need to make sure that you are giving positive affirmations to yourself because they will help with your motivation to exercise and complete your goals. You'll not have any distractions. Block out time in your day for you and only you. You might laugh, but get off work, sit in your car, hide in the bathroom or closet, breathe, and transition from work to family. I suggest you try it.

You can put your affirmations on your fridge, listen in the car, and say them with a positive accountability buddy.

Here are some positive affirmations to uplift your spirit:

1. Every day, I grow more robust and more rigid.
2. I am enough just as I am.
3. I am grateful for the abundance that surrounds me.
4. I am in control of my happiness and well-being.
5. I am worthy of love and happiness.
6. I attract positivity and good energy into my life.
7. I believe in my abilities and trust my intuition.
8. I embrace change and welcome new opportunities.
9. I radiate confidence and positivity.
10. My thoughts are powerful, and I choose to think positively.

Feel free to repeat these or modify them to make them your own!

DAY 9

Cooking Plan and Grocery Store Shopping

Crafting the perfect cooking plan and executing a successful grocery store shopping trip is essential to maintaining a healthy, balanced diet and ensuring a smooth and enjoyable cooking experience. The first step is to carefully consider your weekly meal needs, considering any dietary restrictions, personal preferences, and household schedules. Armed with this information, you can then meticulously plan a varied menu of nutritious and delectable dishes, incorporating a diverse array of fresh produce, lean proteins, whole grains, and heart-healthy fats. With our meal plan firmly in place, the next task is to assemble a comprehensive shopping list, methodically cataloging every ingredient required to bring your culinary vision to life. As you venture forth to the grocery store, it's crucial to approach your shopping expedition with a keen eye and an organized mindset. Navigating the aisles with purpose, you'll deftly locate each item on your list, skillfully selecting the freshest, highest-quality ingredients to stock your kitchen. Throughout this process, it's essential to remain flexible and adaptable, ready to make substitutions or try new ingredients that catch your eye and inspire culinary creativity. By seamlessly blending meal planning and grocery shopping, you'll set the stage for a week of nourishing, delicious home-cooked meals that will delight your taste buds and nourish your body.

It is a great time to create your grocery store list. The grocery list needs to have your list of items. A cooking plan is the best. I am telling you not to go to the grocery store hungry because you will purchase unnecessary items and will not have the items you need to cook your meal. Your grocery list is the best because you will not have to look for things to cook in the last few minutes before work or after leaving your family functions. Ensure you do your cooking plan at the beginning of the week. Monday's menu can be sandwiches, chips, water, or any leftovers from Sunday. On Tuesday, you can make regular, vegan, or veggie lasagna. You can make some good old, dirty rice with salad and bread. For dirty rice, you can add ground beef or ground turkey. You can do this on Thursday or eat a veggie or regular lasagna. On Fridays, it can be a free-for-all because you can have leftovers from the week. You can purchase gift cards for your favorite restaurant. You can give everyone a gift card for their favorite restaurant, and you are not spending cash. You can use gift cards with flights and cruises. One breakfast idea is to boil eggs because they can stay in the refrigerator for up to three days. You can have oatmeal, cereal, or any breakfast before 9 am. You can make the mason jar salad, put it in any refrigerator for up to four days, and take it to work to ensure you have lunch. If you leave the mason jar over four days, check it and ensure the salad is not soggy.

Packing a healthy lunch for yourself and your family is an important task that can significantly impact your overall well-being and nutrition. When preparing a nutritious midday meal, it's crucial to include a balance of essential macronutrients like proteins, complex carbohydrates, and healthy fats. Lean meats, poultry, or plant-based proteins such as beans, lentils, or tofu make excellent protein sources that provide lasting energy and support muscle growth and repair. Pair these with whole grains like brown rice, quinoa, or whole wheat bread to deliver complex carbs that digest slowly and keep you feeling full. Remember to load up on fresh fruits and vegetables, which are brimming with vitamins, minerals, and fiber to support immune function and digestive health. The text below emphasizes incorporating healthy fats from avocado, nuts, seeds, or olive oil to promote heart health and brain function. By enabling a balanced lunch thoughtfully, you'll nourish your body, set a positive example for your family members, and encourage lifelong healthy eating habits. With some meal prep and creativity, packing a nutritious midday meal can be an enjoyable and rewarding task that pays dividends for the whole household.

Pack yourself and your family healthy lunches because it benefits your health and banking account. If they do not eat the lunch, you can still pack it and save it for the future. There are a few things I want to share: Take the boiled eggs and keep them in your refrigerator for up to three days; you can get some mason jars and make different salads. So many recipes online allow you to create a salad and leave it in your refrigerator. The mason jar salads will last up to four days. Your family will start eating those healthy lunches because they will see you are not spending as much money as them, and you'll be able to buy the things you need.

Mason Jar:

Mason jar salads are a fantastic way to prepare healthy, convenient, and delicious meals ahead of time. Here are a few tips and recipes to get you started:

How to Pack a Mason Jar Salad

Dressing: Start with your favorite dressing at the bottom to keep the other ingredients from getting soggy.

Hearty Vegetables: Add sturdy veggies like cucumbers, carrots, and bell peppers.

Proteins: Include proteins such as beans, chicken, or tofu.

Grains: Add grains like quinoa, rice, or pasta.

Greens: Top with leafy greens like spinach, arugula, or lettuce.

Toppings: Finish with nuts, seeds, or cheese.

Recipe Ideas

Greek Salad:

Dressing: Olive oil, lemon juice, oregano

Veggies: Cucumbers, tomatoes, red onion

Protein: Chickpeas

Grains: Quinoa

Greens: Spinach

Toppings: Feta cheese, olives

Southwest Chicken Salad:

Dressing: Chipotle ranch

Veggies: Corn, black beans, bell peppers

Protein: Grilled chicken

Grains: Brown rice

Greens: Romaine lettuce

Toppings: Cheddar cheese, tortilla strips

Caprese Salad:

Dressing: Balsamic vinaigrette

Veggies: Cherry tomatoes

Protein: Mozzarella balls

Greens: Basil leaves, arugula

Toppings: Pine nuts

DAY 10
Date and Cleanse Your Skin

Taking the time to date and cleanse yourself thoughtfully can be a profoundly transformative experience. The act of dating oneself, setting aside dedicated time to nurture and reconnect with the self, is a powerful practice of self-love and self-discovery. It might involve

- treating yourself to a special meal,
- embarking on a solo adventure, or
- simply carving out uninterrupted moments for solitary reflection.

In these private, intentional dates, you have the freedom to explore your innermost thoughts and desires and to check in with your emotional and spiritual well-being without the distractions or expectations of others. Complimenting this self-dating is the cleansing ritual - clearing away the mental, physical, and energetic clutter that can accumulate and weigh us down. It could manifest as a mindful journaling session to purge worries and stresses, a soothing bath infused with therapeutic herbs and oils, or a thorough decluttering of your living space. The cleansing process helps create a sense of lightness and clarity, allowing you to move forward with a renewed focus and purpose. Ultimately, dating and cleansing the self is an investment in your holistic well-being, a way to honor your needs, replenish your resources, and cultivate a deeper, more nourishing relationship with yourself - the most important connection you will ever have.

Day ten is about dating yourself because you can ensure you are being nice to yourself and treating yourself well. You can take yourself to the movie, catch up on any film you've been missing, and take yourself. Some ideas are dating and cleansing yourself regularly, which serve many purposes. Dating helps eliminate potentially harmful substances or thoughts from your body and mind. Removing things that may slow you down can make you feel better mentally and physically.

DAY 11

Date Your Mate

Dating your mate, or one's significant other, is a cherished and time-honored tradition that allows two people in a committed relationship to reconnect, rekindle their passion, and strengthen the bonds of their partnership. Far more than just a casual outing or social engagement, a date with one's mate is a purposeful and intentional act of investing in the health and vitality of the relationship. It provides a dedicated space and time for the couple to step away from the hustle and bustle of daily life, forget about work responsibilities and household chores, and focus on each other. During a date, partners can engage in meaningful conversation, reminisce about cherished memories, try new experiences together, or revel in each other's company. This quality time helps partners remember why they fell in love in the first place, reaffirm their commitment, and leave them feeling refreshed, rejuvenated, and more deeply connected. Whether it's an elaborate night in the town or a simple picnic in the park, date nights allow couples to nurture their relationship, cultivate intimacy, and ensure their love continues to blossom. In an increasingly busy world filled with distractions, setting aside dedicated date time is an invaluable gift that partners can give to one another and to the relationship itself.

It is a chance to write out the date and night of your meeting. We can be monthly or weekly, whatever you need to create the date. You haven't even set up some contacts with your babysitters. You can start saving for the babysitter. You can pick out your favorite outfit for the date night to get you excited about it, and the couples need a little time away. Dating your mate helps strengthen your bond and keep the relationship exciting. It gives you time to connect, communicate, and create new memories. Plus, it can break the routine and remind you why you fell in love in the first place. It's all about fostering intimacy, having fun, and growing together! What's your favorite way to spend time with your partner?

You can take out a favorite family member or friend if you do not have a mate. You can make it an extra special night. The date can be inexpensive, such as a carpet picnic in the house, a date in the park, or watching your favorite movie. If you have someone and you are still dating, you can make it your best night and get to know each other. If you are ready to get married, it is the perfect chance to get to know each other.

Once you start to date again, it will be fun. You can double date with family and friends.

Find fun things to do that make dating your mate an easy habit. You have couples who took up gardening because neither knew anything about the topic. As beginners without prior experience, they embarked on a journey to discover the best ways to garden and perfect timing, wholeheartedly embracing the shared learning experience. The couple joyfully explored local spots that held special significance in their relationship, fostering a deeper connection. You can take up dance lessons, and it is an effortless romance of dancing together.

Venturing into new interests together enriches your shared life and strengthens your bond. Embracing new experiences broadens your horizons and nurtures the growth of your relationship. Nurturing the romance in your marriage requires dedicating time and effort to cherish moments with your spouse. Dating your partner is a beautiful reminder of their value and the importance of your marriage.

Love is an action, and dating your partner provides the perfect opportunity to express your love. Through dating, couples uncover each other's unique qualities, fostering a deeper connection. We are still a family and accumulating abundant shared experiences; my husband and I are still finding one another.

DAY 12

List What You Are Grateful For

A deep gratitude and appreciation can be a truly transformative experience. When we take the time to pause and reflect on the dedications and goodness in our lives, whether it's the support of loved ones, the beauty of the natural world, or even the tiny everyday comforts we often take for granted, it has the power to shift our entire perspective. Cultivating gratitude allows us to shift our focus away from what's lacking or going wrong and instead shine a light on all we must be thankful for. Your mental and emotional shift can have a profound impact, making us feel more content, optimistic, and connected to the world around us. Moreover, research has shown that people who regularly practice gratitude experience greater life satisfaction, stronger relationships, and improved physical and mental health. By taking a moment each day to reflect on the things, people, and experiences we are grateful for, we open ourselves to greater abundance and joy. Ultimately, gratitude is not just a feeling but a way of being that can immensely enrich our lives. On my website, it is a Yearly Gratitude Journal, and it will be great for day 12. The Yearly Gratitude Journal is the ultimate 366-day guide to cultivating gratitude. The self-discovery journal offers daily gratitude prompts to help you focus on being thankful for life's big and small things. By starting each day with a positive mindset and writing down the things you're grateful for, you'll be on your way to a happier and more fulfilling life. Why not invite a friend to join you on this journey? Sharing experiences often leads to a deeper appreciation and enjoyment of them. Make gratitude a habit and start appreciating the gratitude in your life.

Gratitude plays a significant role in self-help and personal development. Here are a few ways it can be beneficial:

- **Improved Mental Health**: Regularly practicing gratitude can reduce stress, anxiety, and depression. It helps shift focus from negative to positive aspects of life.

- **Enhanced Relationships**: Expressing gratitude to others can strengthen connections and foster a sense of community.

- **Increased Strength**: Focusing on what you're thankful for can help you bounce back from setbacks and challenges.

- **Better Self-Esteem**: Acknowledging your achievements and the positive aspects of your life can boost your self-worth.

- **Mindfulness**: Practicing gratitude encourages you to be present and appreciate the small moments, enhancing overall well-being.

To incorporate gratitude into your routine, try keeping a gratitude journal, where you write down things you're thankful for each day or express thanks to someone directly. What are some things you are grateful for? It can be your life, your family, or your friends. Just think of something that you are thankful for when you are grateful. It will help you appreciate things in life.

20 things to be grateful for:

- Anything is possible for you
- Challenges are meant to be conquered by you.
- Each mistake is an opportunity for growth.
- Embracing positivity can enrich every aspect of your life.
- Self-healing is within your reach. Every day holds the promise of new experiences.
- Some people love you
- You are breathing
- You can bring into existence everything you yearn for. Pursuing your passions can lead to abundant wealth.
- You can read this
- You have made it this far
- You can be better than yesterday
- You have the power to become whoever you aspire to be.
- Your creativity knows no bounds.
- Your dreams are attainable
- Your reality is yours to shape.
- Your thoughts are within your control, and you can embrace joy.

For example, practicing gratification and gratitude daily within your routine is okay, which can benefit your mental well-being and overall happiness!

DAY 13

Plan Events with Your Family

It is the perfect time to disconnect from social media. Planning events with your family can be a wonderfully rewarding experience that brings everyone closer together. It starts with brainstorming ideas - a fun day trip to a local museum or zoo, an outdoor picnic in the park, or a cozy movie night at home with homemade snacks. Once you've settled on an activity, the fun begins as you delegate tasks and get everyone involved in the planning process. Younger family members can help make decorations or prepare the food, while older participants may take charge of logistics like transportation or scheduling. The collaborative effort infuses the event with shared purpose and excitement. As the big day arrives, you'll enjoy quality time with your loved ones, making memories that will last a lifetime. Whether trying a new adventure or revisiting a beloved family tradition, planning events together allows you to learn more about each other's interests and create meaningful experiences that strengthen your family bonds. The whole process, from the initial idea to the final celebration, is a beautiful way to build traditions, foster communication, and ensure your family stays connected.

It is time to plan. Working on a family event on Friday nights can be a movie night inside or outside the home or at the drive-in movie. We're planning events with your family. You'll need to ensure you have their plans on your planner. That will be fine, too. The family events can include going to the dental and doctor's offices together.

Planning events with your family can be a great way to bond and create lasting memories!

Here are some ideas for family events you can organize:

1. **Family Game Night**
    - **Activities**: Board games, card games, or video games.
    - **Food**: Make popcorn, order pizza, or have a snack bar.
2. **Outdoor Picnic**
    - **Location**: Local Park or backyard.
    - **Food**: Sandwiches, fruit, and homemade desserts.
    - **Activities**: Frisbee, soccer, or a nature walk.
3. **Movie Marathon**
    - **Theme**: Choose a series or genre (e.g., Disney, classic films).
    - **Setup**: Create a cozy viewing area with blankets and pillows.
    - **Snacks**: Popcorn, candy, and drinks.
4. **Family Potluck Dinner**
    - **Plan**: Each family member brings a dish to share.
    - **Theme**: Choose a cuisine or holiday theme.
    - **Activities**: Share stories or play trivia about the dishes.
5. **Craft Day**
    - **Projects**: DIY crafts like painting, scrapbooking, or building models.
    - **Supplies**: Gather materials beforehand.
    - **Display**: Set up a showcase for everyone's creations.

6. **Family Nature Hike**

    - **Location**: Local trails or nature reserves.

    - **Preparation**: Pack a small backpack with water and snacks.

    - **Activities**: Birdwatching or nature scavenger hunt.

7. **Themed Dinner Night**

    - **Theme**: Italian night, taco night, or a favorite cuisine.

    - **Involvement**: Everyone helps prepare the meal.

    - **Ambiance**: Set the mood with music and decorations.

8. **Volunteer Together**

    - **Choose**: A local charity or community project.

    - **Activities**: Food bank, animal shelter, or community cleanup.

    - **Impact**: Discuss the experience together afterward.

9. **Family Talent Show**

    - **Setup**: Each member performs a talent (singing, dancing, etc.).

    - **Judging**: Family votes for fun categories like "most creative."

    - **Snacks**: Light refreshments for the audience.

10. **Seasonal Celebrations**

    - **Holidays**: Plan specific events around holidays (Halloween, Thanksgiving).

    - **Traditions**: Incorporate family traditions and create new ones.

Tips for Success:

   - **Involve Everyone**: Get input from all family members on activities.

   - **Keep It Flexible**: Be open to changes and adaptations.

   - **Capture Moments**: Take photos or videos to remember the day.

Enjoy your time together! Family nights are so exciting because they bring the family closer.

DAY 14

Dance and stretch for 30 mins

Devoting 30 minutes daily to dance and stretch incredibly positively impacts your physical and mental well-being. Starting with an invigorating dance session gets your blood flowing and muscles moving, increasing your heart rate and releasing endorphins that instantly lift your spirits. Whether you're drawn to the infectious beats of salsa, the fluid movements of contemporary dance, or the lively steps of your favorite choreographed routine, losing yourself in the music and movement is a fantastic way to reduce stress, enhance coordination, and boost cardiovascular health. Transitioning from dance to a comprehensive stretching routine allows your body to slow down, elongate tight muscles, and regain balance. Gentle stretches for the major muscle groups like quads, hamstrings, hips, back, and shoulders help enhance flexibility, joint mobility, and muscle recovery, all while fostering deep relaxation. This holistic practice of dance and stretching keeps your body fit and flexible and offers a precious opportunity to connect with yourself, clear your mind, and realign your energy. Just dedicating about an hour, a day to this simple yet powerful routine can leave you feeling revitalized, centered, and prepared to tackle the rest of your day with a smile.

Get ready to dance and enjoy a 10-minute walk, or why not add an extra 10 minutes to your workout to make it even more enjoyable? Dancing is a fantastic way to involve your family, friends, or social media community and spread joy and laughter. Let's make every moment count and have a blast!

Dancing with family is a joyful way to connect and create lasting memories! Here are a few ideas to make it unique:

1. **Family Dance Party**: Choose a night to blast some favorite tunes and dance around the living room. Everyone can pick their go-to songs!

2. **Dance Challenges**: Have fun with prevalent dance challenges from social media. It's a great way to get everyone involved and laughing.

3. **Themed Nights**: Pick an evening theme—like 80s night or a specific genre—and dress up accordingly. It adds an extra layer of fun!

4. **Family Talent Show**: Each family member can prepare a short dance routine to showcase. Your family can be a great way to encourage creativity and performance.

5. **Learn Together**: Try taking a family dance class online or in person. It could be anything from salsa to hip-hop!

Let's come together to celebrate the happiness of dancing and build stronger connections! I'd love to know—what's your go-to family song for dancing or your preferred dance style?

I enjoy dancing after game night with the family. It is so much fun and puts smiles on everyone's faces. We do not realize we are not using our cell phones, and the night is magical. My favorite genre of music is slower songs.

DAY 15

Have a Good Laugh and Enjoy a Great Movie!

You are watching a good movie, whether a classic comedy or a gripping drama, and it can be a wonderfully rejuvenating experience! If you're looking to unwind, consider a feel-good film or a lighthearted comedy. Watching a good movie can escape reality, immersing yourself in different stories and experiences. It can also evoke emotions, spark imagination, and offer new perspectives. Plus, it's a great way to relax and enjoy quality entertainment! Movies can transport us to different worlds, helping us unwind and experience various emotions. They can also foster connections with others when shared, making for a perfect way to relax and enjoy time with friends or family.

As you immerse yourself in a captivating movie, whether a timeless classic or a compelling drama, you are in for an authentic experience. If you're seeking relaxation, consider immersing yourself in a heartwarming film or an uplifting comedy. Watching a good movie allows you to disconnect from reality and immerse yourself in diverse stories and experiences, triggering emotions and igniting your imagination. Furthermore, it provides fresh perspectives and a fantastic avenue for unwinding and savoring high-quality entertainment. Movies can transport us to alternate realms, enabling us to relax and experience many emotions. Furthermore, when shared, they can foster meaningful connections with others, offering a perfect opportunity to relax and relish moments with friends and family.

Watching a good movie can be a wonderful experience for several reasons:

1. **Entertainment and Relaxation**: Movies provide a great way to unwind and escape daily stress.

2. **Emotional Connection**: Films often evoke strong emotions, whether laughter, tears, or excitement.

3. **Learning and Insight**: Movies can offer new perspectives and insights into cultures, historical events, and human experiences.

4. **Social Connection**: Watching a movie with friends or family can be a bonding experience.

5. **Art Appreciation**: Films are a form of art that combines visual storytelling, music, and performance.

Movies offer a wonderful escape from the demands of everyday life. They evoke many emotions, from joy and amusement to heartfelt tears and exhilaration. Additionally, they can broaden our understanding of various cultures, historical events, and the human condition. Sharing the experience of watching movies with our loved ones provides a unique opportunity for connection and bonding. It's essential to recognize that movies are a captivating fusion of visual narrative, music, and acting - a genuine art form deserving admiration.

As the opening credits roll, the day's stresses start to melt away, replaced by a sense of anticipation and excitement. As the plot unfolds on the screen, the viewer transports to a different world filled with compelling characters, clever dialogue, and moments that elicit laughter, tears, or contemplation. There's something innately human about getting lost in a well-crafted cinematic story, allowing the sights and sounds to wash over you and evoke emotions. Whether it's the infectious cackle of a comedic protagonist or the poignant silence of a tragic scene, the ability of film to connect with our innermost thoughts and feelings is genuinely remarkable. And when the credits finally roll and the lights come up, there's often a palpable sense of having been changed, even if just a little, by the experience. Laughing, crying, or being entertained - the power of an excellent movie to lift our spirits and provide a much-needed respite from the rigors of daily life is a gift to be treasured.

It's about that time to indulge in a comedy film. It's guaranteed to bring out some hearty laughs and provide immense enjoyment. You have various options to catch the movie: you can cozy up at home, head to the nearby theater, purchase the film online, or visit a drive-in theater. Whichever way you choose, don't forget to grab your favorite movie snacks to enhance the experience, whether you're watching at home, at the local theater, or the drive-in.

My favorite is watching a love story.

The reason I live to watch love movies for various reasons:

1. **Emotional Connection**: They resonate with the themes of love, longing, and relationships, often evoking strong emotions.

2. **Escapism**: Love stories break reality, allowing viewers to experience idealized romance.

3. **Relatability**: Many viewers can relate to the characters' experiences, making the stories personal.

4. **Hope and Inspiration**: Love movies often portray positive outcomes, offering hope and inspiration for their lives.

5. **Cultural Reflection**: They can reflect societal norms and values around love and relationships, sparking discussions.

Overall, love movies can be both entertaining and thought-provoking.

DAY 16

Clean the Car & House

Maintaining a clean and well-kept home is essential to personal and domestic care. When learning how to clean your car and home, it is necessary to approach the task with a systematic and thorough mindset. When you leave one room, ensure it is tidy. It will help with the daily cleaning and involve the family in a routine schedule. It involves a multi-step process for the vehicle - first, thoroughly vacuuming the interior to remove any dirt, debris, or crumbs accumulated in the seats, floor mats, and crevices. Next, using a specialized car-safe cleaning solution, wipe down all the surfaces, from the dashboard to the door panels, restoring a fresh, gleaming shine. Don't forget to clean the windows inside and out to ensure optimal visibility. A thorough wash and wax for the exterior will make the car look its best and help protect the paint from the elements. In the home, a comprehensive cleaning regimen is critical. Start by decluttering each room, removing items that do not belong there, and organizing the space. Then, tackle the dusting, wiping down surfaces, and sweeping or vacuuming the floors. Please pay special attention to high-traffic areas and those prone to grime, such as the kitchen and bathrooms, ensuring they are disinfected and sparkling clean. Finally, don't neglect often-overlooked areas like ceiling fans, baseboards, and windowsills. By dedicating time and effort to these cleaning tasks, you can maintain a fresh, inviting, and well-cared-for living environment inside your home and in your vehicle.

It's that time again for some cleaning! It could mean tidying up the living space, decluttering old clothes and shoes, and dusting. You can make any attempts to create a cleaner and more organized home environment will be highly appreciated. Let's tackle tidying, decluttering, and dusting with enthusiasm. The efforts in making your home or space cleaner and more organized are warmly welcomed and genuinely appreciated. Let's make your home a wonderful place to be! Your family can assist you because kids dislike cleaning their rooms.

Cleaning your house and car can be satisfying! Here are some tips to help you get started:

House Cleaning Tips:

1. **Declutter First:** Remove any items that don't belong in each room. It will make the actual cleaning process much more manageable.

2. **Dust and Vacuum:** Dust surfaces and vacuum floors, including under furniture. Remember to dust ceiling fans and light fixtures.

3. **Clean Windows and Mirrors:** Use equal vinegar and water for a streak-free shine.

4. **Kitchen:** Clean countertops, appliances, and sinks. Use baking soda and water to scrub tough stains.

5. **Bathrooms:** Use a bathroom cleaner or a mixture of vinegar and baking soda to clean sinks, toilets, and showers.

6. **Floors:** Mop hard floors with a suitable cleaner. Consider a deep clean with a carpet cleaner or a mixture of vinegar and water for carpets.

Car Cleaning Tips:

Cleaning your car can be a rewarding task, leaving it looking shiny and new. Here's a step-by-step guide to help you get started:

Exterior Cleaning

1. **Gather Supplies**: You'll need car soap, microfiber wash mitts, buckets, a hose, a grit guard, a microfiber drying towel, and wax.

2. **Rinse the Car**: Start by rinsing your car with water to remove dirt and unwanted items.

3. **Wash with Soap**: Use a car-specific soap and a microfiber mitt to wash the vehicle from top to bottom. Do not use dish soap, as it will remove the wax from the car.

4. **Rinse Again**: Rinse off the soap thoroughly.

5. **Dry the Car**: Dry the car with a microfiber towel to prevent water spots.

Interior Cleaning

1. **Remove Trash**: Clear out any trash and personal items from the car.

2. **Vacuum**: Vacuum the seats, floor mats, and carpets.

3. **Clean Surfaces**: Wipe down the dashboard, console, and other surfaces with a microfiber cloth and an appropriate cleaner.

4. **Windows**: Clean the inside of the windows with a glass cleaner.

5. **Condition Leather**: If you have leather seats, use a leather conditioner to keep them supple.

Wheels and Tires

1. **Clean the Wheels**: Scrub the wheels with a cleaner and a brush.

2. **Dress the Tires**: Apply tire dressing to give the tires a shiny finish.

After you clean your car and go home, relax.

Here's a plan to help you rejuvenate:

Morning

1. **Gentle Wake-Up**: Start your day with soft music or natural sounds.

2. **Herbal Tea**: Enjoy a chamomile or lavender tea to set a calming tone.

Mid-Morning

1. **Nature Walk**: Stroll in a nearby park or garden, focusing on your surroundings.

Afternoon

1. **Lunch**: Prepare a light, healthy meal—perhaps a salad with fresh herbs.

2. **Lavender Bath**: Use lavender essential oil or bath salts to create a relaxing bath experience. Dim the lights, light some candles, and soak for 30 minutes.

Evening

1. **Relaxing Activity**: Engage in a calming activity like reading or journaling.

2. **Light Dinner**: Have a simple dinner, like grilled vegetables or a comforting soup.

Night

1. **Bedtime Routine**: Wind down with a few minutes of meditation or deep breathing before bed.

Cleaning your entire home could take about three hours. Every cleaning session is a rewarding and satisfying experience! As you maintain your home, it's crucial to prioritize delivering exceptional quality. Whether you're communicating this to your cleaning service provider or tackling the cleaning yourself, it's important to allocate ample time to address any often-overlooked areas. Aim for outstanding results during each cleaning session, even if time is limited. Both parties will be thrilled to see flawlessly clean rooms and tasks completed perfectly. Consider setting aside approximately 40 minutes for tidying and making beds, 30-45 minutes for sprucing up bathrooms, 45 minutes for the living room, and 40 minutes for the kitchen. Understanding the time required for each area will help you prioritize and give extra attention where it's needed. Let's strive to make every cleaning session a rewarding and satisfying experience!

When considering whether you need to perform a deep clean in certain rooms, it's important to understand the various tasks that can typically be accomplished within three hours. These tasks include:

1. General dusting of furniture
2. Decluttering and organizing scattered items
3. Stripping bed linens and laundering them
4. Washing dishes
5. Dusting kitchen surfaces and appliances
6. Dusting shelves

To ensure efficient cleaning, it's essential to communicate your specific cleaning requirements to your family, regarding of the rooms cleaning throughout the entire house.

Tasks can be prioritized based on specific areas or functions within your home to optimize the three-hour cleaning schedule. Depending on the level of clutter or dust present, each task may take up to 20 minutes or more.

Some of the tasks that can be completed within a three-hour timeframe include:

1. Wiping down countertops
2. Cleaning bathrooms, including bathtubs, shower heads, and toilets
3. Vacuuming
4. Dusting and vacuuming baseboards

5. Wiping kitchen surfaces and washing dishes
6. Mopping floors
7. Laundering clothes
8. Cleaning the fridge and oven

It's important to note that while spending ten minutes cleaning each area may seem quick, accumulating these tasks can quickly consume the entire three hours. Therefore, identifying the areas that require the most attention is crucial for effective time management.

Decluttering is an essential step. It may involve organizing items such as toys, bookstalls, loose change, used clothes, and plates. Minimizing disarray in the home can facilitate focused cleaning and maintenance.

Dust particles, though small, can significantly impact both the cleanliness of your home and your health. Regular dusting should be included in the three-hour cleaning session, ensuring that all critical and visible surfaces are thoroughly dusted from top to bottom. Additionally, washing bedding and curtains, tidying the house, and periodically replacing bed linens are essential for maintaining a clean environment. Investing in environmentally friendly filters and air purifiers can remove dust and promote fresh indoor air quality.

Choosing a portable, affordable, and powerful vacuum cleaner that suits your flooring type is crucial for effective dust and debris removal. Vacuuming should be performed frequently, especially for carpeted floors. High-traffic areas may require daily vacuuming, while less frequented spaces can be vacuumed twice a week. Additionally, regular vacuuming of hard floors is essential, with caution taken to avoid using strong chemicals. Pet owners should prioritize daily vacuuming to minimize dander accumulation.

Wet cleaning involves cleaning bathroom fixtures and windowpanes, which should follow vacuuming. Allowing cleaning sprays to sit for approximately 20 minutes can optimize their effectiveness. For tasks such as eliminating shower soap scum and mold, using vinegar and tea tree oil can provide efficient and immediate results.

Mopping should commence after clearing and sweeping the floor. Mop in sections to prevent grime buildup, ensuring the cleaning liquid adequately covers the desired areas. Wiping the surface three to four times can facilitate thorough cleaning.

DAY 17

Pampering Day

A "Pampering Day" is the perfect opportunity for self-care and relaxation. It's a chance to step away from the hustle and bustle of everyday life and treat yourself to an array of soothing, rejuvenating experiences. The day can begin with a luxurious soak in a warm, fragrant bath, perhaps infused with nourishing oils or calming bath salts that melt away tension and stress. Afterward, the pampering continues with a therapeutic massage, where skilled hands knead and soothe aching muscles, releasing built-up knots and leaving the body feeling weightless. A visit to the salon for a precision haircut, deep conditioning treatment, and expertly applied makeup can have you looking and feeling your absolute best. And a pampering day is complete without some dedicated "me time" - whether curling up with a good book, practicing gentle yoga or meditation, or simply enjoying the peace. The key is to curate a day filled with activities that make you feel refreshed, renewed, and completely at ease. It's a chance to recharge your batteries, reset your mindset, and emerge feeling rejuvenated, radiant, and ready to take on the world again.

You can plan a spa day with yourself or a group you and others will enjoy. You can relax and meditate if you are not in the mood for the spa day. You might not even cook that day or hire a babysitter; it's just something for you. For example, I dedicate my birthday to self-care, a rejuvenating massage, and taking a day off to focus on myself. It's a joyous occasion to embrace my new age and cherish my well-being with the loving support of those around me.

DAY 18

No Excuses

It is a day of no excuses. That simple yet powerful phrase cuts right to the heart of personal accountability and responsibility. It's a direct challenge to the endless litany of justifications, rationalizations, and finger-pointing that often plague our lives and hold us back from reaching our full potential. The "no excuses" mindset requires us to take responsibility for our circumstances, choices, and the resulting outcomes, no matter how uncomfortable or inconvenient. This mindset helps us appreciate the small things in life. It requires us to stop making excuses, to stop blaming external factors beyond our control, and to start taking decisive action to overcome obstacles and achieve our goals. At its core, "no excuses" is a rejection of victimhood and a declaration of agency - an affirmation that we are the captains of our ships, the architects of our lives. It's a call to shed our self-imposed limitations, to silence the voice of doubt and fear, and to push past our comfort zones with unwavering determination. Adopting a "no excuses" approach unlocks a wellspring of power, resourcefulness, and resilience within ourselves.

We stop making excuses and start making progress. We stop pointing fingers and start taking steps. We stop dwelling on what we can't control and focus on what we can. It's a mindset shift that turns obstacles into opportunities and setbacks into springboards for growth. Embracing "no excuses" isn't always easy, but it is always worth it - for it is the surest path to actualizing our biggest dreams and boldest visions for ourselves.

There is no excuse for anything. It is not a day to complain about anything. You want to be so positive about everything. If your child comes home with bad grades, then be nice. If your coworker is asking 1 million questions and you're repeating yourself. It is ok. Today is your workout day, so make a note of it. You do not have to tell anyone you are making a note, but make sure you do it for yourself. It is time to work out. If it's not Tuesday, if it's your day to do your fire hydrants, or if you need to do some jumping jacks or walking for 30 minutes, make sure you do it. I am wholeheartedly devoted to the process of writing my book and determined to overcome any obstacles that may come my way. My unwavering commitment drives me to see this project through to completion, and my greatest wish is that the passion I pour into my writing will be reflected in the joy you experience while reading it.

DAY 19

Step Out for a 15-Minute Nature Walk

Taking a brief 15-minute stroll through nature can be a wonderfully rejuvenating experience. Step outside and immerse yourself in the sights, sounds, and sensations of the natural world around you. As you begin your walk, notice how the sunlight filters through the leaves overhead, casting a warm, mottled glow on the ground below. Listen closely, and you may hear the melodic chirping of birds, the rustling of wind through the trees, or the buzzing of industrious insects going about their business. Breathe deeply and fill your lungs with the crisp, fresh air, feeling it revitalize your body. Keep your eyes peeled for signs of life - perhaps you'll spot a squirrel scurrying up a trunk, a butterfly fluttering among the flowers, or a rabbit darting through the underbrush. Pay attention to the diverse textures and colors surrounding you, from the rough bark of tree trunks to the delicate petals of blooming plants. Even a brief foray into nature can have a remarkably calming, therapeutic effect, allowing you to momentarily disconnect from the stresses of everyday life and reconnect with the beauty and serenity of the great outdoors. So, the next time you need a quick mental health break, consider stepping outside for a refreshing 15-minute nature walk.

What do you think about your health? If your health is excellent, write a goal to keep it immaculate. If you have some work to do with your health, work on it and write it down. If you do not complete your goals, encourage yourself, rewrite them yearly, and keep at them until they are complete. Improving your health could increase your chances of living longer and decrease stressors. But stress plays a vital role in your health. A suggestion for your health goal is to complete joyful exercises such as yoga, speedwalking, or things to improve your overall health.

Walking in the neighborhood, you can see many different parts of nature. Absolutely! A neighborhood walk can reveal various natural elements, from trees and shrubs to flowers and birds. You might notice seasonal changes, like vibrant fall leaves or budding spring flowers, as well as nature's different textures and colors. Observing the wildlife, like squirrels or birds, adds to the experience, too. It's a great way to connect with the environment!

If you cannot get outside, sit on the porch and enjoy nature! Sitting on the patio can be a perfect way to enjoy nature from home. You can hear birds chirping, watch the wind rustle through the leaves, and feel the sun's warmth. It's a peaceful way to connect with your surroundings and unwind. Even small details, like the patterns of clouds or the colors of the flowers, can be a source of inspiration and tranquility.

If you're in a colder state, enjoy a cozy indoor activity or take a stroll around your home. If you're in a warmer climate, staying hydrated is a great idea, as is heading out for a refreshing nature walk. Stay safe and enjoy the wonderful outdoors!

DAY 20

Call a Positive Person

Calling a positive person can be a rejuvenating and uplifting experience. These individuals radiate an infectious energy, their presence lifting your spirits and reminding you of the brighter side of life. When you connect with a positive person, you find yourself drawn into their optimistic outlook, as they effortlessly redirect your focus away from the stresses and struggles of the day. They can identify the silver linings, the opportunities for growth, and the reasons to be grateful, even during challenges. Their words flow with encouragement, their laughter is genuine and bright, and their unwavering faith in better days ahead is reassuring. Spending time with a positive person can feel like stepping into the sunlight after a long period of darkness - their warmth envelops you, and you can't help but feel your mood shift and your perspective expand. Their company's problems shrink, worries fade, and the path forward seems more evident. Calling a positive person is like recharging your emotional batteries, leaving you inspired, motivated, and ready to tackle whatever lies ahead with a renewed sense of purpose and possibility. You don't have to limit yourself to just one favorite person. Surround yourself with a circle of positive individuals who bring out the best in you. You must do the same thing.

Do you surround yourself with positivity? I asked myself the same thing. If your circle is unfavorable, rethink the individuals in your process and re-create it. Is the issue you? I took the time to date myself and love myself before I could love anyone. I am a work-in-process. To me, achieving the little tasks is enormous, and I will pat myself on the back.

If you don't love yourself, then who will love you? I went to the movies, lunches, and dinner with myself and loved it. Take time to get to know yourself and surround yourself with positive individuals. It is okay to have a bad day but turn it into a joyous one. My joyful day is opening the window with wind and sunshine on my skin, brisk walking, listening or dancing to my favorite artist, and spending time with family and friends.

It sounds like you're looking for ways to describe a positive person! Here are some traits that typically define a positive individual:

- **Cheerful**: Has a happy and bright disposition.
- **Compassionate**: Shows empathy and concern for others.
- **Encouraging**: Inspires others to do their best.
- **Optimistic**: Always looking on the bright side of things.
- **Resilient**: Able to bounce back from setbacks.
- **Upbeat**: Full of energy and enthusiasm.

It is time to call a positive person. Calling a positive person will make you feel positive, and you can get the positive information you need. The positive person can be multiple people or individuals, but it ensures you have your positive person.

DAY 21

Rest Day and Positive Affirmations

A well-deserved rest day is crucial to any fitness or training regimen, allowing the body and mind to recuperate and recharge after intense physical exertion. During these vital breaks, the muscles can repair any micro tears that have occurred, replenish depleted energy stores, and adapt to the stresses placed upon them. This recovery process is essential for building strength, endurance, and resilience, as the body requires adequate rest to super-compensate and come back stronger than before. Rest days also provide a mental respite, allowing the mind to step away from the rigors of a demanding workout schedule and avoid the burnout that can occur with excessive training. By listening to the body's signals and honoring the need for periodic rest, individuals can optimize their fitness journey, avoiding injury and maintaining the motivation and energy to push themselves to new heights on their next training day. The benefits of a well-timed rest day extend far beyond the physical realm, fostering a healthy balance between activity and recovery that supports overall health and well-being.

You can schedule a rest day. People may laugh but sit on your couch and enjoy your favorite beverage. I'm talking about taking a real break—no cooking, cleaning, or running errands. If possible, arrange to have someone else take care of the kids and your partner for a few hours so you have time to yourself, even if it's not the entire day.

Say three things and give positive affirmations about yourself.

As a confident and capable individual, I am proud to say three positive things about myself. First and foremost, I am a highly adaptable person who can thrive in various situations. When you are faced with a new challenge at work or an unexpected change in my personal life, I have the resilience and problem-solving skills to navigate any obstacles that come my way. Secondly, I am a compassionate and empathetic individual who genuinely cares about the well-being of others. I consciously try to be a supportive friend, a considerate family member, and an understanding colleague, always striving to lend a helping hand or an attentive ear when someone is in need. Finally, I deeply value my creativity and innovative mindset, allowing me to approach tasks and projects uniquely. I constantly seek new ways to think outside the box and develop original solutions, fueled by a relentless curiosity to learn and grow. These core qualities - adaptability, compassion, and creativity - are the foundation upon which I have built a fulfilling and meaningful life. I am genuinely grateful for their positive impact on my personal and professional endeavors.

It is time to stay true to yourself and say three positive things about yourself, such as "I am beautiful," "I am successful," and "I can't do it." Saying positive things about yourself will make you feel great, and you can succeed in your goals. The positive affirmations will do wonders for you and your self-esteem. If someone is making you mad, say positive affirmations, and you can improve your day. You can tell an unlimited number of positive affirmations to yourself.

DAY 22
Automate Savings and Retirement

Automating your savings and retirement planning is an incredibly effective way to ensure a secure financial future. You can effortlessly build up your nest egg without thinking about it by setting up automatic transfers from your regular checking account into dedicated savings and investment accounts. The "set it and forget it" approach takes willpower and discipline out of the equation, allowing your money to grow steadily through the power of compounding interest over time. Whether you funnel a portion of each paycheck into a savings plan or automatically transfer a fixed amount to a high-yield savings account each month, automating these critical financial tasks means you don't have to remember to make the transfers yourself. It reduces the risk of procrastination or forgetfulness, derailing your savings goals. Plus, by automating your retirement contributions, you benefit from the tax advantages of these accounts, further accelerating your path to a comfortable retirement. You must ensure you have enough in your primary checking account to cover your bills and everyday expenses. The rest will be automatically diverted into the appropriate savings and investment vehicles. This hands-off approach takes the guesswork and effort out of building wealth, allowing your money to work for you even when you're not actively considering it.

At the start of each new year, I always tell myself that I will diligently save a specific amount of money from my income. Your savings are less by September, and you want to save **$100.00 monthly**. In your savings, you should have 900 dollars ($100.00 x 9 months=$900). You only want to have an emergency savings account for emergencies.

You should only have an emergency savings account for emergencies. You should always have at least $2,000 in your emergency savings banking account. You can keep building on it and not have it below $2,000. If you have a car, please price a set of tires, and you will be amazed at the price.

You always want at least $500-$1,000 in your savings banking. Some examples of when to use your emergency savings include new car engines, car tires, career loss, and many more. Non-emergency items include a new pair of shoes due to attending a local concert and a new pair of jeans because they are cute, and you get the concept of the emergency and non-emergency items.

You want to have zero debt because everyone wants to be debt-free. Here, the number of years when you want to be debt-free, such as one, two, five, or six years from now, with the name of the goal. Do you want to be debt-free? Such as clearing a mortgage, student loan, or credit card? Once you pay off the smallest to the most significant deficit, give yourself a high five because the debt is complete. Your next step is to take the debt money and place it into a savings account or an investment. For example, if your debt totaled **$300**, you want to take the money and open a savings or investment account.

If you are planning to retire in 15 years, you want to make sure you have enough money to pay taxes on your retirement money and still live. You'll still have to pay taxes on your retirement account; please check with your accountant, 401k team, banking, and others who manage your retirement account.

Automating your savings is a smart way to ensure you consistently set aside money without thinking about it. Here are a few steps to get started:

1. **Set a Savings Goal**: Determine how much you want to save and by when. It could be for an emergency fund, a vacation, or a big purchase.

2. **Choose a Savings Account**: If you need a dedicated savings account, open one. Look for accounts with reasonable interest rates and low fees.

3. **Automate Transfers**: Set up automatic transfers from your checking account to your savings account. You can do this through your bank's online banking platform. Decide the amount and frequency (e.g., weekly, bi-weekly, or monthly).

4. **Use Savings Apps**: Consider using apps that help automate savings. Apps can round up your purchases, save spare change, or set aside small amounts regularly.

5. **Review and Adjust**: Periodically review your savings plan and adjust the amount if needed. As your income or expenses change, you might want to increase or decrease your savings rate.

Automating your savings can help you build a financial cushion with minimal effort.

DAY 23

Disconnect and Unplug for 30 Minutes a Day

In today's hyper-connected, digital-driven world, intentionally disconnecting and unplugging each day is more important than ever. Dedicating just 30 minutes away from the constant notifications, alerts, and endless screens scrolling can provide a much-needed respite and reset for the mind and body. During this technology-free interlude, you can find solace in being present, grounded in the here and now, without the distractions and demands of the online realm. Use a half-hour to engage in a mindful activity that brings you joy and fulfillment, whether reading a book, going for a stroll, practicing gentle yoga or meditation, or simply sitting in quiet contemplation. Disconnect from the digital tether and reconnect with yourself, your immediate surroundings, and the natural world's rhythms. This grief yet rejuvenating break will leave you feeling more focused, centered, and better equipped to tackle the remainder of your day with clarity and composure rather than the frazzled state that can easily creep in when not allowing the resetting of your brain. Make unplugging a consistent habit, and you'll be amazed by its profound impact on your overall well-being.

Prioritize your well-being by allocating a specific weekly time for relaxation and unwinding. Consider setting aside at least 30 minutes to disconnect from social media and electronic devices. Use this precious time to play board games, which can effectively help reduce stress. Keep an eye out for special holiday offers on board games to enhance your collection and provide more options for leisure and entertainment.

It is essential to prioritize personal well-being by allocating dedicated weekly time for relaxation and revitalization. Consider scheduling at least 30 minutes to disconnect from ineffective things. It is valuable time can be utilized to engage in the pleasure of playing board games, a proven method for reducing stress and embracing enjoyment. Watch for special holiday promotions on family games to expand your collection and diversify leisure and entertainment options. Investing in personal well-being in this conscientious manner is genuinely beneficial and indispensable.

Taking a break from technology and unplugging is a fantastic way to escape the hustle and bustle of daily life. However, it can be quite a challenge for individuals to recognize the impact of excessive phone use and constant web browsing. The allure of social media and continuous news updates often distract us from the beauty of the world around us.

Unplugging offers the opportunity to set aside technology and reconnect with loved ones briefly. Many individuals are grappling with the negative consequences of prolonged screen time. Even when enjoying e-books on tablets, the screen's light can lead to eye strain, headaches, and disrupted sleep.

Taking a break sounds like a great idea! It's essential to recharge. Here are a few suggestions for your 30-minute unplug:

1. **Go for a walk**: Fresh air and a change of scenery can do wonders.
2. **Listen to music**: Enjoy some of your favorite tunes.
3. **Meditate**: A few minutes of mindfulness can help clear your mind.
4. **Read a book**: Dive into a good story or learn something new.
5. **Stretch or light exercise**: It can boost your energy and mood.

DAY 24

Forgive Others

Forgiveness holds transformative power, healing deep emotional wounds, restoring fractured relationships, and liberating us from resentment and bitterness. When we choose to forgive, we are not minimizing or excusing the wrongdoing of others; instead, we are choosing to unshackle ourselves from the negative emotions that threaten to consume us when we harbor anger and pain. It is a deliberate and mindful decision to relinquish our grip on the past, embrace progress, and direct our focus toward the potential for personal growth and deeper understanding.

Forgiveness is not always easy; it is a journey that requires courage, empathy, and willingness to see beyond our perspectives. It means acknowledging the pain we have experienced but then choosing to let it go, extend compassion, and recognize the humanity in those who have hurt us. It can be incredibly challenging when the transgressions are significant or the wounds are deep, but it is in these moments that the power of forgiveness shines brightest. By forgiving, we free ourselves from the weight of negativity and open the door to healing, reconciliation, and even personal transformation.

Ultimately, forgiveness is a gift we give to ourselves. It allows us to move forward with a lighter heart, cultivate more positive relationships, and find greater peace and well-being. It is a testament to our strength, resilience, and capacity for growth and a skill that we can all work to develop and refine over time. By racing forgiveness, we liberate ourselves and contribute to a more compassionate and understanding world.

Forgiving yourself can be liberating because it allows you to let go of the burden you've been carrying. When you forgive yourself, you free yourself from self-imposed guilt and open up the possibility for self-compassion and self-growth. Furthermore, once you have forgiven others, you'll find it much easier to communicate openly and honestly with them. Forgiveness paves the way for healthier and more transparent relationships, leading to better understanding and empathy between individuals.

Forgiving others can be a powerful and healing process. It often involves letting go of resentment and anger, which can benefit your mental and emotional well-being. Here are a few steps that might help:

1. **Acknowledge Your Feelings**: It's essential to recognize and accept your emotions. Allow yourself to feel hurt, anger, or sadness before moving towards forgiveness.

2. **Communicate**: Have an open and honest conversation with the person who hurt you. Express your feelings calmly and listen to their side of the story.

3. **Empathize with the Other Person**: Try to see the situation from the other person's perspective. It doesn't mean you must agree with their actions, but understanding their motives can sometimes make forgiving easier.

4. **Let Go**: Forgiveness is about releasing the negative emotions' hold on you. It doesn't mean forgetting or excusing the behavior; it means freeing yourself from resentment.

5. **Seek Support**: Sometimes, talking to a friend, family member, or therapist can provide the support you need to process your feelings and move toward forgiveness.

6. **Understand the Impact**: Reflect on how holding onto grudges affects you. Often, it can lead to stress and negatively impact your health.

Forgiving others can be difficult and emotionally taxing, but it often leads to a deep sense of inner peace and fosters the growth of more robust and more harmonious relationships.

DAY 25

Treat Your Body and Relax

Treating your body with care and finding ways to relax are essential for your physical and mental well-being. Nurturing your body through soothing and rejuvenating activities can profoundly impact your overall health and happiness. It might involve indulging in a luxurious bubble bath infused with calming essential oils, allowing the warm water to envelop you and wash away the day's stresses. Or it means treating yourself to a massage, where trained hands knead away the tension in your muscles, releasing built-up pockets of tightness and restoring a sense of ease throughout your frame. Relaxation can also come in gentle yoga flows, where you methodically move through poses that lengthen and stretch your limbs, your breath becoming a steady, meditative anchor. Even simply carving out time to curl up with a good book, getting lost in an engaging story that transports you to another world, can be a wonderfully refreshing act of self-care. No matter the specific activity, the key is to approach it with intention, allowing yourself to fully disengage from the demands of daily life and focus solely on the present moment. When you prioritize treating your body with kindness and making space for relaxation, you'll feel rejuvenated, refreshed, and better equipped to tackle life's challenges with clarity and poise.

Treating your body and relaxation is a plus! Our bodies go through so much. It is like running a marathon and not stopping to get a glass of water to sleep. We're just running, running, running. Once you realize you have planned for so long, your body will tell you to slow down and take care of me first. It's essential to take time for self-care and relaxation. When was the last time you treated yourself to a facial, massage, or a visit to the hair salon? It may be time to schedule some much-needed time for yourself. Whether you're busy raising a family, juggling work and school, or just managing the demands of daily life, it's crucial to prioritize self-care. You serve to take a break and unwind. Don't wait until you are completely burnt out to prioritize your well-being. Consider scheduling a spa day, a night out, or just a few moments of relaxation at home. Take time to transition from work to home life each day, indulge in a warm bath, listen to soothing music, and find moments to relax. And members should plan a vacation, whether with your family or just for yourself. Self-care is essential for maintaining balance and overall well-being.

Taking time to treat your body and relax is essential for overall well-being. Here are a few ideas to help you unwind and rejuvenate:

1. **Practice Mindfulness and Meditation**
    - **Mindfulness**: Spend a few minutes focusing on your breath and being present. It can help reduce stress and improve mental clarity.
    - **Meditation**: Guided meditation apps like Headspace or Calm can be beneficial.

2. **Enjoy a Warm Bath**
    - **Epsom Salt Bath**: Add Epsom salts to your bath to help relax your muscles.

- **Aromatherapy**: Use essential oils like lavender or eucalyptus to create a calming atmosphere.

3. Gentle Exercise

- **Yoga**: Practicing yoga can help stretch and relax your muscles while calming your mind.
- **Walking**: A leisurely walk in nature can be very soothing.

4. Pamper Yourself

- **Skincare Routine**: Take some time to pamper your skin with a face mask or a gentle exfoliation.
- **Massage**: Treat yourself to a professional massage or use a foam roller at home if possible.

5. Disconnect from Technology

- **Digital Detox**: Spend 30 minutes away from screens to give your mind a break. Disconnecting from technology could be a great way to relax.

6. Listen to Music or Read a Book

- **Music**: Create a playlist of your favorite relaxing songs.
- **Reading**: Dive into a good book to escape and unwind.

7. Stay Hydrated and Eat Well

- **Hydration**: Drink plenty of water throughout the day.
- **Healthy Snacks**: Enjoy some fresh fruits or nuts to nourish your body.

DAY 26

Refrain from Eating Past 8 pm

The adage "don't eat past 8 pm" is a piece of health advice that has become increasingly common in recent years, and for good reason. The human body operates on a circadian rhythm, a natural cycle that governs our sleep-wake patterns and various physiological processes. Consuming food late in the evening can disrupt this delicate rhythm, leading to many potential issues. The digestive system typically winds down as bedtime approaches, making it less efficient at breaking down and metabolizing the food we consume. Therefore, it can result in slower digestion, feelings of discomfort or bloating, and even weight gain over time as the body struggles to process the excess calories properly.

Additionally, eating close to bedtime has been linked to poorer sleep quality, as the body's energy is diverted away from rest and restoration towards the demands of digestion. It can leave us feeling sluggish and tired the next day. Perhaps most importantly, studies have shown that late-night snacking is often associated with a higher intake of unhealthy, calorie-dense foods with little nutritional value. By setting a firm cutoff time for eating, typically around 8 pm, we can avoid these pitfalls and support our overall health and well-being through more mindful eating habits and better-aligned circadian rhythms.

On Day 26 of the program, it's essential to refrain from eating anything after 8 pm. I understand that some of you may feel dissatisfied with this guideline, especially if you tend to prepare meals after 8:00 pm. However, adhering to this rule is crucial for achieving your best physical appearance and optimal performance. Many of us often overlook the significance of following these guidelines. Therefore, I encourage you to plan your meals and grocery shop over the weekend to set yourself up for success.

The idea of not eating past 8 pm is quite common, especially regarding weight management and digestion. However, the science behind it is more nuanced. You can avoid eating late due to managing weight, digestion, and metabolism. A tip is to keep portions small, and an option is to have lighter meals in the evening. Ultimately, it's more about what you eat and how much you eat rather than the exact time. If you stick to balanced meals and healthy choices, eating after 8 pm isn't necessarily a problem.

As we mature, it's essential to prioritize avoiding morning fatigue by being mindful of late-night meals that might not be good for our stomachs.

DAY 27

Meditate in the am and Before Bed

Incorporating meditation into your morning and before-bed routine can be a profoundly transformative practice that yields numerous benefits for your mental, physical, and emotional well-being. Start your day with a mindfulness meditation session, which allows you to set a calm, centered tone and cultivate greater focus and clarity as you navigate the day ahead. Taking just 10-15 minutes to sit quietly, turn your attention inward, and gently observe your breath can help you feel more grounded, present, and equipped to handle any challenges or stressors that may arise. Similarly, winding down your evenings with a meditation practice can be an invaluable tool for relieving stress, releasing built-up tension in the body, and preparing the mind for restful, restorative sleep. As you settle into a comfortable seated position, slowly turn your awareness to the sensations of the breath moving in and out and let go of the thoughts and worries of the day, you'll find your body and mind gradually entering a state of deep relaxation. Over time, this consistent meditation habit can lead to heightened self-awareness, improved emotional regulation, and an enhanced capacity for resilience – all of which can have a profoundly positive impact on your overall quality of life. So, whether you're looking to start your mornings with clarity and intention or wind down your nights with peace and tranquility, making time for meditation at both ends of the day can be a truly transformative practice.

Meditate in the morning and before you go to bed. It will help you start and end your day. Get your family in meditation because it will benefit the family. The family may not like the meditation, but you will have everyone come and join it. Meditation does not have to have an age, a number, ethnicity, or anything else. You can meditate with your neighbor, family, friends, or whoever wants to get involved and meditate with you.

Incorporating meditation into your morning and evening routines can have many benefits. Let's take a closer look at the advantages of each:

Morning Meditation:

- **Begin Your Day with Tranquility:** By meditating in the morning, you can establish a serene and peaceful mindset, which can assist you in managing stress more effectively throughout the day.

- **Enhanced Focus:** Morning meditation has the potential to boost your ability to concentrate and be more productive as you navigate through your daily tasks.

Evening Meditation:

- **Relax and Unwind:** Meditation in the evening allows you to unwind from the day's events and alleviate accumulated stress.

- **Improved Sleep Quality:** Evening meditation can improve sleep by soothing your mind and body before bedtime, leading to a more restful and rejuvenating slumber.

For example, meditation is my favorite part because it decreases my blood pressure, ensures my calmness, and improves my day and sleep.

DAY 28

Read an Enjoyable Book

The vast and enchanting world of literature beckons those who have yet to experience the joy of losing themselves in the pages of a mesmerizing book. Luckily, numerous digital pathways are available for accessing these literary marvels, ranging from online platforms to electronic reading devices. Delving into a well-crafted book offers many benefits, including stress relief and deepening knowledge. It's truly captivating! It expands one's vocabulary, contributes to well-being, and enhances communication skills. Whether you're lost in the pages of a physical book or engrossed in an audiobook on your commute or at the doctor's office, the love for literature knows no bounds.

Reading can improve relationships because you can share your favorite books with family, friends, and others. It can also increase understanding. In the "What Is Your Motivation" journal, the flower on the cover is a Black-Eyed Susan, symbolizing encouragement, motivation, and impartiality, or the Foxtail lily, representing endurance. The pink roses on the "Yearly Gratitude Journal for Personal Growth and Self-Discovery" cover symbolize gratitude.

When I sit down at my keyboard, I desire to craft meaningful, helpful, inspiring, and supportive content. Whether you're seeking encouragement, facing challenges, or simply looking for a great book to share, I'm here to provide the information you need with enthusiasm and optimism.

DAY 29

Complete Your To-do List

Completing your to-do list can be a tremendously satisfying and empowering experience. It's the culmination of diligent planning and hard work, a tangible representation of your productivity and focus. As you methodically work through each task, checking the task off individually, you can feel a growing sense of accomplishment and control over your day. The feeling of crossing the final item off that list is akin to reaching the summit of a challenging hike - you've put in the effort, overcome any obstacles, and now you get to bask in the rewards of your labor. Not only does completing your to-do list provide that immediate gratification, but it also sets you up for continued success. With our most pressing tasks handled, you can focus on bigger-picture goals, knowing you've laid a solid foundation for progress. And there's an undeniable boost to your mood and confidence that comes from being able to look back on all you've accomplished. The to-do list is a humble but powerful tool - a simple organizational system that, when used effectively, can streamline your workflow, enhance your productivity, and leave you with a true sense of achievement.

The to-do list is a valuable tool for organizing and managing all the tasks and responsibilities in your life. If you encounter challenging or awkward tasks you can't handle alone, don't hesitate to seek assistance from a family member, friend, or anyone willing to help.

DAY 30

Limit Social Media

In today's digital age, the constant influx of social media has become a ubiquitous part of daily life for many individuals. However, research has shown that excessive social media usage can have detrimental effects on mental health, productivity, and overall well-being. It is, therefore, crucial to carefully consider one's social media habits and establish healthy boundaries. Limiting social media time can help reduce feelings of anxiety, depression, and FOMO (fear of missing out) that often arise from endlessly scrolling through carefully curated feeds and comparing oneself to the idealized lives of others online.

Additionally, stepping away from social platforms allows for more focused attention and deeper engagement in real-world activities, hobbies, and face-to-face interactions - all essential for maintaining a balanced lifestyle. By setting specific time limits for social media use, individuals can reclaim their mental space, boost productivity, and cultivate more meaningful connections in the physical world. Ultimately, moderating one's social media consumption is an essential act of self-care that can lead to improved mental health, increased presence, and a greater sense of overall life satisfaction.

Hey there! I get where you're coming from, but hear me out—cutting back on social media can do wonders for your well-being and peace of mind. Next time you hop on, try setting a timer, jotting down the time and date in your journals without peeking, and see how it goes. You're doing great with your Yearly Gratitude and What Is Your Motivation Journal, and I believe this small change can significantly impact you. If you do not have a copy of the Journals, they are available on my website at wondraspencer.com. Keep up the excellent work!

When you have completed your social media review, I want you to look at how much time you have taken to review social media. Over the next few days, I want you to reduce your time by 10 minutes during the first week. I want you to reduce your time by 20 minutes for the second week. In the third week, I want you to reduce your time by 30 minutes. The goal for social media is to spend less than two hours daily. For my math people, you have seven days a week, and 7×2 is 14, so you spend 14 hours weekly on social media. It is 30 days monthly, and you spend 60 hours on social media. In a year, if you spend two hours on social media in a 365 day, you have spent 730 hours on social media. For a family of four, yearly, you spend 2,920 hours on social media, for a couple 1,460 hours.

You can do much more in your day with the two hours you spend on social media. If you limit your hours to two hours, you want to limit your family. You can reward yourself for decreasing your social media time. During the week, you cannot be on your social media. You can limit social media when it is your dinner time and spend quality time with the family. You can improve your well-being with your compression if you're feeling lonely, missing out, or having negative feelings and urgency. The family can play board games, beach day, add nature walks and picnics, and enjoy each other's company. Our family cherishes the time spent together, whether unwinding with a movie, engaging in exciting game sessions, or simply enjoying a meal. These moments with our loved ones hold immense value for us.

One of our cherished family traditions involves refraining from social media on Sunday mornings until noon. This practice allows us to unwind and strengthen our family bonds. Additionally, we have a delightful tradition of dedicating Friday evenings to lively family game nights. This weekly tradition is something we eagerly anticipate as it unites us for some meaningful quality time together.

CELEBRATION
Take time to Celebrate your Progress!

Celebrating how far you have come is a powerful act of self-reflection and appreciation. It's so easy to get caught up in the day-to-day grind, always striving for the next goal or milestone, that we often fail to pause and take stock of just how much progress we've made. But taking the time to do so can be incredibly rewarding and motivating. Think back to where you were a year ago or five years ago - the challenges you've overcome, the skills you've developed, the growth you've experienced. It's easy to get discouraged by how much further you feel you must go, but if you shift your perspective and focus on how far you've already come, you'll likely be amazed. Maybe you've finally started that business you've been dreaming of made significant strides in your career, or made meaningful improvements to your physical or mental health. Or it's smaller, subtler changes - you've become a better communicator, learned to set healthier boundaries, and discovered new passions and interests. Whatever it is, give yourself credit. Celebrate the wins, no matter how big or small. Reflect on how much you've grown and evolved. Take a moment to feel proud of yourself and your accomplishments. Doing so can provide a profound sense of gratitude, renewed motivation, and faith in your ability to keep moving forward and reach even greater heights.

It's time to rejoice and celebrate your achievement! You've completed the 30-day challenge, and I hope this experience has equipped you with valuable tools for this new phase in your life. Remember to use these effective methods as a helpful resource whenever you feel you're not reaching your full potential.

Consider marking a special occasion with these five methods:

- Preparing a delicious meal that you love.
- Hosting a lively gathering with friends and family.
- Treat yourself to something you've always wanted.
- Indulging in a day of self-care and relaxation.
- Take some time to rest and rejuvenate.
- Cooking Your Favorite Meal
- Party
- Purchase Your Favorite Item
- Pampering day
- Rest

Cooking your favorite meal can be an enriching and relaxing experience. Taking the time to select fresh, high-quality ingredients carefully and then thoughtfully prepare them with skill and attention to detail allows you to engage in a delightful act of self-care. The rhythmic chopping of vegetables, the sizzle of meat in the pan, and the aromatic blend of spices wafting through the kitchen all contribute to a meditative, almost therapeutic process. As you lose yourself in the systematic steps of the recipe, your focus narrows to the present moment, allowing you to set aside any stresses or worries temporarily. The result - a masterfully crafted dish that tantalizes the senses and nourishes both body and soul - provides a profound sense of accomplishment. Sitting down to savor each flavorful bite can feel like an indulgent treat, a way to treat yourself with the kindness and care you deserve. Cooking your favorite meal is more than just preparing food - it's a chance to slow down, reconnect with yourself, and engage in self-love.

Hosting a lively party is an excellent way to unite people, create cherished memories, and inject much-needed fun and excitement into your life. Planning alone can be enormously rewarding as you tap into your creativity to craft the perfect theme, menu, and ambiance. Meticulously selecting the decor, music, and refreshments lets you infuse your style and flair into the event. But the true magic happens when your guests arrive, mingling and laughing as they connect. Watching new and old friends engage in animated conversation, share stories, and make merry fills the air with electric energy. There's something so rejuvenating about basking in the warmth of community, of allowing yourself to be fully present and in the moment. And when the party winds down, you're left with a heart full of joy and a renewed appreciation for the essential people in your life. Hosting a gathering is more than just throwing an event - it's an opportunity to cultivate joy, strengthen bonds, and nourish the soul.

Indulging in purchasing your favorite item can be a delightful form of self-care and a chance to treat yourself with kindness. Whether it's a beautifully crafted piece of clothing that makes you feel confident and beautiful, a high-quality kitchen gadget that streamlines your cooking process, or a sumptuous beauty product that helps you pamper your skin, the act of selecting and acquiring something you truly desire can be tremendously satisfying. The participation of its arrival, the excitement of unboxing your new treasure, and the joy you feel when using or wearing it all contribute to an overall experience of personal fulfillment. But the benefits go beyond just the material item itself. Allowing yourself to indulge in something that brings you happiness can be a powerful statement of self-love and a reminder to prioritize your needs and preferences. Engaging in this purposeful, mindful consumption can be a therapeutic way to cultivate a deeper appreciation for what you value most.

Dedicating a day to pampering and self-care can be a transformative experience, allowing you to pause daily life's demands and focus solely on your well-being. Whether indulging in a luxurious spa treatment, losing yourself in a good book, or simply carving out uninterrupted time for rest, this intentional self-nurturing can have profound effects. Disrupting from work, chores, and other obligations and directing your energy inward can help you feel rejuvenated, grounded, and more in touch with your authentic self. Engaging in activities that bring you joy, comfort, and a sense of peace - a soothing bath, a meditative walk in nature, or a decadent homemade meal - can help alleviate stress, boost your mood, refresh you, and restore. A pampering day is about pampering the body, mind, and spirit. It's a chance to slow down, reflect, and nourish yourself on a deep, holistic level - an investment in your overall well-being that pays dividends far beyond the immediate experience.

Resting and recharging is essential to living a balanced, fulfilling life. In our fast-paced, often overwhelming world, it's easy to become caught up in a perpetual cycle of work, obligations, and external demands, leaving little room for true respite and rejuvenation. However, intentionally carving out rest periods is beneficial and necessary for maintaining our physical, mental, and emotional well-being. Whether it's an afternoon spent curled up with a good book, an evening devoted to unplugging from technology and engaging in a calming hobby, or a weekend getaway to recharge in nature, these moments of rest and restoration allow us to press pause, quiet the noise, and reconnect with ourselves. Deciding away from the hustle and bustle of permitting ourselves to "be" rather than "do" can help alleviate stress, boost creativity, and foster greater inner peace and clarity. Resting is not a luxury but a fundamental need - a way to refill our emotional and mental reserves so that we can show up as our best selves, both for ourselves and the people and responsibilities in our lives.

Here's a 30-day plan to help you transform into a new version of yourself:

Week 1: Set the Foundation

1. **Day 1:** Define your goals. Write down what you want to achieve in 30 days.

2. **Day 2:** Create a vision board or list of affirmations.

3. **Day 3:** Declutter your space. Remove items that no longer serve you.

4. **Day 4:** Establish a morning routine that energizes you.

5. **Day 5:** Write in your What Is Your Motivational or Yearly Gratitude journal. Write about your thoughts and feelings.

6. **Day 6:** Identify and eliminate one harmful habit.
7. **Day 7:** Plan healthy meals for the week ahead.

Week 2: Build Healthy Habits

8. **Day 8:** Begin a daily exercise routine, even if it's just a short walk.

9. **Day 9:** Practice mindfulness or meditation for 5-10 minutes.

10. **Day 10:** Read a book that inspires or teaches something new.

11. **Day 11:** Connect with a friend or family member for support.

12. **Day 12:** Try a new hobby or activity that excites you.

13. **Day 13:** Focus on hydration—drink plenty of water.

14. **Day 14:** Reflect on your progress so far. Adjust goals if necessary.

Week 3: Deepen Your Growth

15. **Day 15:** Set aside time for self-care. Do something just for you.

16. **Day 16:** Learn a new skill online or through a workshop.

17. **Day 17:** Volunteer or help someone in your community.

18. **Day 18:** Reduce screen time. Engage more in real-life activities.

19. **Day 19:** Experiment with a new recipe that aligns with your health goals.

20. **Day 20:** Practice gratitude. Write down three things you're grateful for.

21. **Day 21:** Evaluate your progress and celebrate small wins.

Week 4: Sustain and Share

22. **Day 22:** Develop a weekly planning habit to stay organized.

23. **Day 23:** Continue exercising and eating healthy.

24. **Day 24:** Share your journey with others. Inspire someone else.

25. **Day 25:** Identify areas for further improvement and set long-term goals.

26. **Day 26:** Revisit your vision board and update it if necessary.

27. **Day 27:** Reflect on what you've learned about yourself this month.

28. **Day 28:** Create a list of your read books

29. **Day 29:** Plan for challenges you might face after this month.

30. **Day 30:** Limit Social Media and Celebrate your transformation! Reflect on your journey and set intentions for the future.

Stay consistent, and remember that transformation is a continuous journey!

Plan of Action

Hey there! A friendly reminder: You're on an incredible journey to becoming the best version of yourself. Surround yourself with positive, like-minded people, and let's motivate each other! I'm thrilled to share the techniques I've learned to inspire and support you. In 30 days, you can transform into a new and improved version of yourself by practicing patience, self-love, staying hydrated, exercising, meditating, and getting enough sleep. Thank you for taking the time to read my book – it means a lot. Please spread the word and embrace the fantastic new you! Stay tuned for more exciting book sessions on my website and social media. I can't wait to connect with you there!